DIVIDED

Published in the United Kingdom by Divided in 2019.

Divided Publishing
251 Avenue Louise, 2nd floor
1050 Brussels
Belgium

https://divided.online

Copyright © Anna Zett, 2019

All rights reserved. No part of this book may be reproduced or transmitted by any means without prior permission of the publisher.

Front cover design by Michael Salu
Printed by Graphius Brussels

2nd edition, 2022

ISBN 978-1-9164250-3-3

Anna Zett

ARTIFICIAL GUT FEELING

Letter to Frau Lieder	9
I've Got the Power, Agathe Bauer	19
Taube	24
agf	29
Artificial Gut Feeling	33
ACh	44
Fist to Brain	51
A Situation	57
Nothing Left Undone	78
Incarnations	83

Letter to Frau Lieder

Frau Lieder has died. I did not know her, she lived in the village. We walk through the house with a few relatives. Why did she live alone? Was she an independent woman? She also seems to have been very conservative. She said at some point that she was the only one who associated her depression with 1989. Apparently, she had never talked to anyone about it before. In fact, this woman wasn't actually Frau Lieder. Now I feel sorry for her.

Hello Frau Lieder,

Lately, I have been thinking about you more often. I don't know your first name; maybe I knew it once and forgot it again. It could be that your name starts with an A, like mine, or with an M, which is perhaps a little more probable, or with a C. I can rule out its starting with Z. You are between fifty-five and seventy years old today. Maybe you are already dead, like quite a few of your generation. In which case, this letter will not reach you.

    I remember in 1990 I walked along a certain street everyday on my way to school, past the kindergarten where you worked until 1989. When I walked down this street, I would ask myself: what will I do if I meet you outside? Will I run away? Will I freeze? Or will I say hello normally? And how will you react? Will I even recognise you? After some time, I was sure I wouldn't recognise you. Your appearance and your voice were eventually erased from my memory. You could have sat next to me on the tram and I wouldn't have noticed you. I'm afraid you retained in this way some power over me, incognito. Not only did you disappear, but my memory plunged you into anonymity and I lost your trace there. Whether or not you were still in town, I hid you inside me. I kept you like an important document one puts in a special place so as not to forget it, one that won't be found again precisely because one has never kept anything of importance in this impractical place before. My body served as your perfect hideaway.

Frau Lieder is my dance teacher. She gives a workshop as part of a larger event that has to do with the digestive organs. We also spend the night there. I take part in the workshops but I don't do the last session, it's something with singing and jumping. I go to my room to roll a joint. Frau Lieder follows me later to check up on me. Oh, no, I didn't know that this was the last session. It turns out the person I talk to is not Frau Lieder at all. I get sad and say, "But we will get together again?" "Yes, there is still going to be a round of talks," she replies.

Frau Lieder, do you remember what happened between us? I would like to ask if you still remember who you wanted to be for the children. Do you still know what it felt like to be someone to whom the state had granted free use of any contactless form of violence? Have you ever wondered what it was, exactly, that you wanted from me – or for me? I could well imagine you never identified your own desires and actions as sadistic. I remember my parents mentioning at some point that you went into the leather goods business afterwards. You quit your job in the kindergarten after the opening of the border, or maybe you had to leave. In any case, you were suddenly gone and you started selling handbags made from crocodile and snake leather (real or fake). That is all I know about your career.

We are in a more or less self-organised seminar group, in a fight-or-flight situation, in an adventurous landscape. Frau Lieder, a young woman from Russia, writes something. The writing becomes scrawly, running diagonally across the paper, and blood starts dripping while she writes, two drops, but they are not coming from the finger, but from me, or from the image.

I'm writing this letter because I'd like to talk to you about sadism. There are various uses of the word "sadistic". They differ, first of all, in terms of whether or not sadism is linked to sexual pleasure. In my memory, nothing happened between us that I would associate with sexuality. I would describe our relationship as purely institutional, more or less impersonal. Between us, there was hardly any touch at all. Isn't it strange that you tormented people to whom you weren't emotionally or sexually connected or dependent upon? By your order, movement was forbidden during the midday nap. Everyone had to close their eyes for the entire length of the nap. Those who opened their eyes were insulted and punished. You sat there to guard our nap, you didn't sit there to protect us. I find it difficult to imagine relationships you might have had outside work, in your personal life. Perhaps my behaviour was only a superficial trigger for your punishments, and it had nothing to do with me. In those moments, perhaps you were somewhere else with your feelings – with a lover? Did you have someone with whom you were tender or passionate? In any case, I can't remember any emotion you might have expressed to me over the course of those three years.

Frau Lieder and I find ourselves going home together again. The mood is playful, the erotic communication works perfectly and Frau Lieder says, with a certain astonishment in tone, "You are different than before, much more determined." I answer, demonstratively unimpressed, "Back then I was afraid of you." It's a simple sentence, much simpler than the truth. In bed, in the grey light of a Berlin morning, I say to Frau Lieder, "Wait, it's strange." "What is it?" "No, it's too strange." "Say, I want to know," he says. Maybe he thinks I'm going to say "I love you", or something like that. But I say: "It is as if you suddenly have no face. Your face is gone." And then we had to stop fucking for a moment because his face was gone. I had to try to kiss an empty head so that the face would come back. Some other face came.

Lieder, although our relationship was a purely institutional one, it still sometimes felt as if I was addressed personally when you coerced my obedience. I remember, for example, how you placed me with my cutlery and plate of lunch at a small table in the hallway and made the children from all the other rooms on the corridor form a group around me, including kids who barely knew me. Then you instructed everyone to point at me with their index fingers and then to wipe this finger in my direction with the index finger of the other hand. A rhythmic amplification of the pointing, so to speak, while singing "neh-ne-ne-neh-ne". And all that just to get me to scrape my plate.

You always liked to direct highly dramatic scenes like that one, in which we were both supposed to play a role. The outcome of these scenes was not open at all, rather was always predetermined by you. Whenever you set up such a scene, for a short moment it certainly felt like we had a relationship, it felt like we had something to do with one another. Yet the interesting thing (and this is what I really want to tell you, after all these years) is that as soon as such a scene was set in motion – once I was sitting there with my meal; or with my red plastic cup of boiled milk with skin; or standing with my face to the corner; or lying on my flat bed in the toilet – you were gone. I was neither angry nor afraid of you. I wasn't thinking about you at all. I was alone in those places. You didn't really exist, you had somehow wiped yourself out through your abuse of power. I had nothing at all to do with you. The children sang: "Shame on you! Shame on you! Everybody sees you!" But the children were just some choir and you, Frau Lieder, were no more. I guess there was not much left of me either, in these moments. Perhaps I was keeping myself busy with practical questions: what will happen if I don't finish up my plate, don't drink up my milk, what if I don't take a single sip, not a single bite, how long can I bear to be excluded from play and from the group, is there a way to get out of this situation, when will all this be over?

Of course, all that happened a long time ago. Who knows how often situations like that occurred, how our dynamic developed over the years, how it really felt. I just want to tell you that you actually didn't get any closer to me in those heightened moments. That might be the difference from the lustful sadism in situations of sexual or creative intimacy. Powerful gestures can bring two people very close together, but only under the condition that both are present with their consciousness and old enough to choose whether they want to participate in intense, borderline-existential powerplay. Most likely, you didn't even want to get close to me. You were just going by the book, trying to properly discipline children, teach them the basic principles of what the government had defined as socialist morality. You were entitled to represent the state, truth, order, peace, life, work, future, punishment, mankind and the group. I was simply at your mercy. But the fact I was at your mercy had no meaning at the time, neither I nor anyone else knew about it. I did not tell my mother about what happened between us. It was not until 1989, when the border opened and you were suddenly gone, that I told someone.

I meet Frau Lieder one summer in Brandenburg, at the garden party of a friend's aunt. She is our mutual acquaintance. We sleep in the same bed. We spend the whole evening in disagreements and quarrels. Now we lie opposite each other and I actually want to touch him, but I can't. Suddenly he opens his eyes, we look at each other, quiet, in a stable lateral position. The gaze lasts long enough. I realise, it's time. After all these years, I finally look Frau Lieder in the eye, we recognise each other and then nothing happens.

The important difference between the two of us is that you have no reason to write to me. I am certainly the only one of us who still thinks of us today. This has to do with the fact that I was a child, one child among many, and you were an adult. You left a mark on me, I probably didn't leave one on you. Our relationship is asymmetrical. There has never been a dialogue between us. In our city, when I was a teenager, I once threw a message in a bottle into the river. It was a dramatic moment. I can't remember what was written on the paper, but I'm sure it didn't contain any particularly tempting offers of contact. Text, desperately thrown into the world, without an address, without any particular imaginary reader in mind, is pointless. It means nothing. Perhaps a letter is an inappropriate format, both for reaching out to an unknown person and for reaching out to someone I don't really remember, like you. When I try to think of you, I find nothing concrete. The details have faded. The thought of you mainly consists of homeless text, and this text tends to fall back onto itself until it collapses. Sometimes a remnant of this thought continues to move through my nervous system in a different form. Sometimes I feel my body, not as in the teachings of meditation and mindfulness, but in a very different way. I feel my body from within; I feel something in my belly that is not part of the normal digestive process; I feel some kind of substance, maybe even a living being, an artificial living being in my guts.

This being is able to transform movement into speech. It winds itself about inside me like a thick snake and I have to use all my strength to let it spin and do what it does. When I wilfully try to stop it, it begins to whisper words to me and that is even more unpleasant. If I were to associate this gut feeling with an emotion, I would say disgust.

But this disgust is not directly linked to your name. Your name is associated only with stories, familiar narratives of an asymmetrical power struggle that no-one won; with spatial fragments, the cold stone floor, corrugated tiles under bare feet, the smell after someone shat themselves and it wasn't cleaned up during the entire nap for educational reasons, a fragment of the street entrance of the kindergarten seen from the inside. Do you remember? The groups of children, sorted by age, started at the top and then moved one floor down each year. Once we had finished with the mezzanine, we finally reached the door. I don't remember the soldier and peace songs we sang, but I read they were required, so most probably they were sung.

Frau Lieder has died and we are at the funeral. I am not sad and try to refuse the ritual. But the group is more powerful than me and it is more powerful than the mother and so in the end I give my condolences to the relatives and then escape the situation as if I had done something terrible.

In recent years many books have been published on the subject of the former German Democratic Republic. *Who We Are*, for example, by Jana Hensel and Wolfgang Engler, or *The East Germans*. Do you read such books? I do identify as an East German and I do find all of this very interesting, yet only up until the moment I remember that, theoretically, you are also included in this category. When I say "we" and when, by that, I mean "East Germans", I include both of us! I find this idea rather disgusting and wonder whether I should leave this category to you or whether I should try instead to exclude you from it using a rhetorical trick. I could say, for example, that your cruelty does not belong to the GDR but is to be understood as a late effect of the Nazi atrocities. I am sure the Nazi regime haunts your family history in some way or another. It definitely haunts mine. But, as a kindergarten teacher, you would surely refuse any link to that past.

In 1986, the year I was handed over to you, new guidelines for national child education were published. The Council of Ministers stipulated that children should "learn more in kindergarten about how the people of their home town lived and worked in earlier times, how they fought for a better life and against war and fascism. They should know that there are no exploiters and fascists in the GDR, as there are in the Federal Republic of Germany". Since it was impossible for fascists and exploiters to appear in the GDR, someone like you would probably not agree to interpret your actions as a Nazi spectre or as a return to fascist violence. What you did would have been fully in line with the socialist ideal, since you were only doing what all kindergarten teachers were allowed and supposed to do in the name of education. My answer to this would be: OK. I believe that whatever you did was entirely reasonable within the cosmology of the GDR, this brave new world that had risen from the ruins of the war and that ceased to exist thirty years ago. I was the one who failed to adapt. I leave the GDR and the general category of East Germanness to you. I'll find myself a new minority of origin. That's definitely possible and it's probably for the best.

At present, I often encounter the assessment that East Germans unfortunately stylise themselves as victims time and again, as a collective of victims. Together they are either victims of the Stasi, the party, the authorities, the government, West Germany, the *Treuhand*, the media, so-called foreigners, or even all of that at the same time. Do you sympathise with this idea? Are you tempted to associate yourself with a collective of victims, possibly as a replacement for the lost community, the lost *Volk*, perhaps even the long-lost *Führer*? I don't expect you to answer this. I know that, for the people of the GDR, it was hard to say "I". One may well desire to be relieved from this new duty to learn how to say "I" successfully, in relationships, on the market. One may need to find one's way back to a state in which responsibility for one's suffering is not found in one's own life, in humanity, in nature or in chance, but in an imagined authority. One may long for relief and refuse to acknowledge one's own vulnerability or one's narcissistic fantasies of greatness. One may desire to project these unconscious fantasies onto a nation, or half a nation, instead. One may also feel the need to remember a person like you – a real-life fucked-up authority figure named Lieder.

I take the ferry, but not to another country. I cross the border of my supposed strength and reach a point where I am infinitely weak, but not yet completely gone. There I can't say no, there I can't answer at all, there I've got used to participating on a transitional basis. There I have to learn to speak again and again. My animal body must learn to say no and yes, not years later, but exactly at the moment when a decision is made. It must distinguish itself from the world and become an individual, responsible for every single one of its decisions, liable as an autonomous ego.

Frau Lieder, I have one more question: do you think your torturous methods took power from me, or empowered me, eventually? In the past, I always thought you staged my exclusion in order to weld the rest of the group into a collective. What happened to me in the process was more or less irrelevant. I was just the deterrent example, the warning to everyone, the interchangeable victim – until it was someone else's turn. But maybe that is the wrong interpretation.

Perhaps you isolated me from the group and punished me in front of everyone because you had in fact chosen me as the one to whom you would give a particularly profound and detailed lesson in your techniques of touchless violence. Perhaps you wanted to teach me something very special and considered me a suitable master student for your hardest lessons. Alas, the state you represented happened to collapse and you could not complete your plan. You ran off and were replaced by another kindergarten teacher, a funny older woman named Quack, with black and grey hair all the way down to her bottom, who was not so familiar with your special methods. We lost sight of each other. Naturally, I didn't miss you. I didn't know that it had been your secret plan to give me a final, resounding lesson at the end of my training, which would show me what had been the point of all the agony, endurance, perseverance. No-one told me it had been your plan to grant me a prize for my desperate resistance, or at least an honourable mention, before you sent me off to school. That's the romantic version of the story.

Frau Lieder walks through the park. Suddenly a boy comes running to her and says, anxiously: "There is a bad dog over there, help me, I am afraid. Can you walk beside me?" Frau Lieder: "Yes, I can." They walk next to each other to the exit of the park, then they say goodbye. Frau Lieder was tall and adult, the boy was small, a child. They didn't know each other, their relationship was purely institutional, there was nothing to dis-

cuss between them. Frau Lieder was proud of herself because she knew she had done the right thing. Luckily, they both had to walk in different directions after the task was completed.

Back then you had power over me, now I have power over myself. I also have power over others – at least temporarily – when I influence people who are open to me in professional or personal contexts. But it is strange, it seems that the more others open up to me, the more alienated I feel from my own will to power. The more my power is wanted, the more I get the feeling that power is actually indistinguishable from care. When in a position of power, I am required to take care of those who are open to me or weaker than me. I must nourish them, strengthen them, make space for them. To be charged with this kind of power seems rather exhausting. Protecting and supporting others is an extremely demanding job. The strangest thing about our power struggle was the recent realisation that you didn't need to enter into a struggle at all. You already had all the power. You were an adult surrounded by small kids. Your contract was unlimited, nobody controlled you, there was no evaluation of your methods.

    I would like to ask if you were sure all resistance was futile. Did you violently provoke my resistance in the blind certainty that you had not only the right but the means to defeat any resistance whatsoever? Frankly, I believe you were not at all that sure of your authority. Your use of force implies you were in combat mode. For some reason, you felt compelled to put your power at risk again and again, like a boxer who must enter the ring time and time again to hold her title. In boxing, though, the opponents are equal and compete against one another in the same weight class. As an adult woman, you chose to challenge a three-to-six-year-old girl. Through your theatrical acts of violence, you were choosing to put yourself at risk, at least theoretically. In practice, I am not sure what effect my resistance had on you. In the nihilist version of the story, you never asked yourself how you would like to use the power you were institutionally granted. Your job was boring and you waged war against the kids just for the thrill of it. There simply was no ultimate goal of your attacks. You, yourself, were the end that justified the means. I don't know exactly why I think this, but I guess the main reason you raised me into your opponent was the loneliness you felt up there. However, it is not in my interest to investigate the details of your loneliness, current or past.

Frau Lieder takes a fasting cure, alone. At first, she slowly reduces her consumption of rabbit hearts, chicken liver, aspic, scalded sausage, smoked pork, bacon, sour eggs in mustard sauce, barley soup, potatoes with curd cheese and boiled milk with skin. Step by step, she quits alcohol, coffee and cigarettes. She buys a pack of detox tea and an irrigator for complete bowel emptying. She gets castor oil, swallows a tablespoon full, shakes herself to disgust, goes to the bathroom and closes the door.

Frau Lieder, I'm glad I don't have to understand you. It suits you well, being a fiction I can empathise with as far as I want to, and no further.

Best wishes,

Anna

I've Got the Power, Agathe Bauer

My earliest memory of Agathe Bauer is from my childhood, around the time when my drawings began no longer to resemble modernist art, but also hadn't yet started to look like failed attempts at depicting an ideal world realistically. I definitely hadn't yet been taught how to visually represent three-dimensional space, and it was years before I was able to draw hands. Possibly this memory formed in the year of the state's termination (1989–1990, the year before I started school), though there is no way to find out whether that's the truth.

I only know that one night I was lying in bed and heard the voice of Agathe Bauer talking to me from inside my ears. I knew she wasn't actually there, I knew her voice was just in my head, yet undeniably she was speaking to me and this was not the first time. Here she was again, speaking and xxx-splaining. As always, I didn't reply. I listened, as I would listen to unknown adults, to audio plays or to people on television. Now, the problem was that Agathe Bauer didn't mean well. I could tell from the way she was speaking, she was here to talk me into something, not so much in the sense of persuasion, more in the sense of forcing me to understand something.

How does a person force another to understand? Let's say A wants to transfer a package of information to B, without B having requested it. If the dialogue is taking place between living people in real space and time, the easiest way for A to make B understand anything is for B already to trust A due to an existing relationship – family tie, friendship, comradeship – which is untroubled by personal conflict. What if there is no such relationship between A and B? Unless society is going through a massive transformation or a revolutionary process at the time, B will likely understand A if A is older or more confident than B or if A is positioned above B, either by institutional position or by locally relevant social binaries like gender, race, class, sexuality, ability, religion, political affiliation, popularity, visual appeal, etc. Unfortunately, it is nearly impossible to acquire these privileges spontaneously. What does A do, in the case of A's failing to fulfil all or some of the above criteria and still desiring to pass a package of information to B, without B having requested it? A very common strategy of spontaneous one-way communication is physical or symbolic aggression. To make up for missing trust or missing authority, A might try to communicate in an aggressive or arrogant tone of voice, to mock, verbally insult or threaten B with moral punishment (for example, in the afterlife) in order to forcefully transmit their information. All of these approaches, however, are very risky. As much as A may successfully humiliate B and thus force them to listen out of fear, A may also destroy any remaining or potential trust − and trust is definitely the most helpful companion on the long and complex road towards making oneself understood. Other strategies may be less risky, more secretive or more complex. They are more difficult to xxx-splain.

To strategically switch between giving and withdrawing affection is commonly practised among caregivers. Although this strategy can be very frustrating and painful for B, it doesn't seem to disrupt trust as much as open aggression does. It is risky in another way, however, as it leaves negative feelings stored in randomly assigned places in B's body, accessible only to fictitious creatures and ghosts, and the consequences for A might be delayed by years, even decades. The least risky and most long-term-oriented strategy is for A to do nothing but listen to B, consistently creating space for B to develop trust. Eventually, years later, when the time has come, A may carefully hint at something and B will immediately understand, even if it is not at all in B's interests to do so. Obviously, this approach requires a lot of skill and patience and may not be suitable to everyone. The latter strategy is one I only recently discovered, in a book about ancient Chinese political diplomacy. Reading about a classical text attributed to Guiguzi, I was surprised to learn that trust could be treated not as a fragile and authentic social tie but as a tool for strategic emotional manipulation.

Did Agathe Bauer use any of these strategies? It is difficult to describe and even harder to remember what it was about her one-way dialogue that made me resist its symbolic flow of information. There is a German proverb: *Wer nicht hören will muss fühlen* ("One who does not want to hear must feel"). It was omnipresent during those dreamy years around the state's termination. Cited by all kinds of adults and repeated by the kids, it meant: if trust does not make One obey Another, Another will resort to other methods to get a message across. Could it be that it wasn't that Agathe Bauer had bad intentions, but that my childish refusal to hear made her voice become threatening, made it seem so physical and sensual, in a horrific way?

Agathe Bauer did not have a body, she was clearly just a voice, and somehow she didn't even sound like a human being. Her voice was distorted, as if it was being transmitted through an electronic device. She was speaking and I was listening. In this way, the relationship was obvious and clear, yet on a symbolic level nothing was clear between us. Agathe Bauer and I were playing an excruciating game. Her tone indicated she had power over me and she had a lot of information to pass on but, though I (think I) tried, there was no way to understand what she was saying. The words were rushing, falling forward, and the sentences were formulated in such an indirect way that it was impossible for me to get the message. Sometimes it was impossible to grasp anything at all. Did she speak the same language as me? Why would I have a voice in my head that speaks an unintelligible language? Her voice was powerful in a sick way, not in a pleasant way, and it was vibrating all over me, from my guts to my brain and back again. Somehow it contained zero symbolic information. Sometimes it felt like she threatened me with punishment but I didn't understand what that punishment would be. I felt that she had knowledge I didn't possess and refused to disclose it to me, or I was stubbornly resisting my own ability to hear.

All's well that starts well, and what never starts, will never end. Years later, I reconnected with Agathe Bauer in a club called *Arbeitskreis für Jenseitskontakte* ("Working Group for Contacting the Beyond"), where my collaborator and I were making recordings for an experimental radio play. I didn't meet her physically – Agathe Bauer doesn't have a body – but we reconnected on another plane. The working group met every two weeks in the cellar of a villa in Berlin-Zehlendorf to search the waves between radio channels for messages from loved ones or other important people who weren't alive anymore. In the beginning, they met in facilities associated with the Catholic Church, but since the church doesn't officially approve of spiritualism, or any technique that enables people to make contact with dead relatives, they were eventually asked to meet elsewhere. The head of the club was Michael, a retired patrol cop who had spent most of his professional life communicating through the police radio. Some of the other members had worked in telecommunications back in the day, another was a retired miner and another a factory worker.

During each regular meeting, they would sit around a table, the ex-cop would turn the knob of the radio looking for a suitable noise, and when he found one the group would try to distinguish intelligible words, names and sentences. Everyone had their own ghosts to talk to, so normally they were simply listening and recording for some time, until someone would say: "I heard something!" In case it wasn't clear right away what the voices had said and to whom they had been speaking, the cop would take the recording home, cut it into pieces and run it through quality-reducing converters in order to remove distracting remnants of actual human voices and, if this wasn't enough, he would also try playing it backwards. At the next meeting, he would present and explain his findings aided by a subtitled audio-video presentation. When my collaborator and I returned for the second round of our oracle, Michael gave us one such a presentation. Throughout the evening we all got a chance to laugh quite a bit because spiritualism can be a very joyful religious practice. At the same time, I experienced a gentle yet very uncanny mixture of nausea and mental pain. The policeman's edit of our ghost-recording sounded shockingly similar to the unforgotten memory of Agathe Bauer.

Guided by the conceptual framework of our radio play project, we had agreed beforehand to attribute all of the ghost-recordings to the voices of Joan of Arc (a voice-hearing warrior and the Catholic patron saint of radio) and of Nikola Tesla (a pigeon-loving loner and the official inventor of radio technology). For the recording session, each of us turned to one of these two historical figures with a personal question and, in the final radio play, we wove the results into a bigger narrative about the two characters, associating them with all kinds of written texts, improvised dialogue and music. Sitting around the table with the people of *Arbeitskreis für Jenseitskontakte*, ears open, ready to listen and make sound recordings, I wouldn't say I was interested in re-experiencing the nauseous presence of my childhood spectre. Yet, there she was again, speaking and not making sense.

Listening to her voice twenty-five years after we first connected still didn't result in her message getting across. This time, however, I was not alone and – to my great relief – I noticed that our relationship had changed. I could have used this rare occasion to listen to my haunted voice on repeat, with the goal of dissecting and properly analysing its content with the help of experts, but, actually, I had a better plan for her nonsense. My collaborator and I were equipped with a narrative framework that already included the presence of meaningless voices – a very open framework, where any sound could be framed, named and linked to a story, even a sound that, in itself, was completely meaningless. So, in the very moment of our adult reconnection, Agathe Bauer and I missed each other again. It wasn't her this time who claimed to speak, while I silently resisted hearing. There was no need for me to insist on the meaninglessness of her authoritative laments and hideous xxx-splanations. Our roles had been swapped and it was Agathe Bauer who now insisted on unintelligibility, on being made out of fragments, while I assumed the right to freely interpret her, to integrate her into a story that was, at least partly, made up. I had come here to listen, to appropriate ghosts, and – luckily – I had grown unable to hear anything that didn't already make sense to me.

Taube

Friedenstaube, Brieftaube, Ringeltaube, Turteltaube, Felsentaube, Haustaube, Straßentaube. Es *gibt viele Sorten von Tauben. In der Biologie werden 42 Gattungen und 300 Arten unterschieden. Auf Schwedisch heißt die Taube* duva, *auf Russisch* golub, *auf Spanisch* paloma, *auf Arabisch* hamama, *auf Hebräisch* jonah, *auf Chinesisch* gēzi.

There is no English translation for this thing. Instead of one word, there are two equally widely used words with two very different networks of association: *dove* and *pigeon*.

A *Taube* is one of the characters in the radio play I worked on over the last couple of months, to be broadcast on national public radio in Germany. I would like to introduce this character to you, but given this is taking place in English, I will first have to deal with the dilemma of translation.

The most inclusive and complex translation would be to create a new word based on both meanings: *pigeon-dove*. Suddenly, a pigeon-dove lands on your windowsill, it looks like it has an important message to convey. You get out of bed and walk towards the window, careful not to scare away the pigeon-dove.

I spelled the new word with a hyphen between *pigeon* and *dove*, but it could also be spelled with a slash, an underscore or, alternatively, an asterisk, like the one sometimes used in German to conjoin masculine, feminine and all other genders into one inclusive term. Some of these spellings are more unusual than others, more academic-looking or more disturbing to conservatives. The hyphen definitely has the highest potential for remaining unnoticed. My problem, though, is that none of these spelling tricks fix the underlying sonic issue. The new word sounds very artificial. Instead of a word that refers to an animal, it sounds more like a band name or the working title for an art project. Basically, it sounds made up. Due to lack of public attention to the pigeon-dove problem, I don't believe it will enter an English dictionary anytime soon. Stylistically, this word sounds indecisive and, in my story, would serve as a narrative spoiler. So, I don't love the composite and will have to use one of the two conventional translations. But which shall I choose?

There are many reasons for choosing *dove*. The first is autobiographical. I learned this word many years before

I learned the word pigeon, possibly because of its etymological link to the German word *Taube*. *Dove* belongs to the realm of myths and fairy tales and comes with lots of positive connotations.

In Eurafricasian religions, doves have served as messengers of life and peace for thousands of years. Most famously, they are mentioned in a story shared by the three Abrahamic religions in which a dove delivers an important message after a disastrous flood. The flood is caused by God's rage, His will to punish, destroy and wipe out all people for their misbehaviour (which was, according to the ancient Ethiopian branch of Christianity, caused by some disloyal angels who had sex with people and taught them how to make art). But Noah has been warned (also by God). He builds a huge ark for his family and every other kind of land animal in order to survive this God-made catastrophe. The ark cruises over the flooded earth, with no plants, only animals on board. At some point, a dove is sent out to look for land and one day it returns carrying a fresh branch from an olive tree in its mouth. Noah understands that if plant life has returned, it means the earth has too, and if the earth has returned, it means the conflict between God, the people and creation is over, so it is peace now. "Thank you for this message," says Noah to the dove.

A few thousand years later, this cosmological incident made it into Unicode's emoji collection. Do all users, all over the world, read the white-bird-with-green-branch emoji as a symbol of peace? We can start from there in our text messages and see where it takes us.

The dove symbol, however, is very old, it is older than its whiteness and greenness. Even the story of the flood had already been told and written in various languages and scriptures and in all kinds of versions, referring to a few different gods, before it made it into the Christian Bible, into my memory, into Wikipedia, into this text, into my mouth.

I wouldn't insist that what follows is a true story, but within some feminist circles it is by now an urban legend of sorts. Sources from the ancient Sumerian civilisation, located in southern Mesopotamia, what is now Iraq, point towards the dove not only as a symbol of peace but as a symbol of the sexual aspect of one of their most powerful gods, Inanna, a very competitive, occasionally gender-bending deity, a.k.a.

the god/dess of war and love. Inanna was always depicted in the company of doves – which are pigeons, but I'll stick to the word dove for now, since that is what they became in the Bible. The dove is said to have been the only sacrificial animal in Sumer that wasn't a mammal, which is explained by its very early domestication for agricultural purposes. But the farm birds' sexual connotations and Inanna's power to balance the opposing forces of fertility and destruction were abandoned in translation as new kings conquered old kings, and as more strictly patriarchal groups living by animal herding continued telling the story. While the Sumerian deity Inanna was demonised in this process, Inanna's attribute – the dove – initially remained an important sacrificial animal. Yet, as the dove was later integrated into the new monotheist religion, the whole associative network around this symbol changed. Its association with female sexuality was twisted and replaced by the inverse – an association with immateriality and ascetic morality.

Eventually this deep symbolic twist lead to the Christian paradox of the motherfucking Holy Spirit – which is not supposed to have a body at all, but which when it is depicted appears as a dove. The Holy Spirit is one of the three aspects of the Christian God and it is hardly ever mentioned. One of the few things it is known for is having impregnated the mother of God immaterially, without involving any sexual act nor any menstrual cycle, thereby making it possible for God to symbolically father Himself. In the German Democratic Republic and other post-war, post-Christian, supposedly pre-communist societies, the dove's ancient paradoxical charge was once again twisted around itself several times, leading to an ubiquity of empty dove images, which propagated the pacifist mindset of a deeply paranoid and authoritarian surveillance state.

You are about to approach the dove that has landed on your windowsill. You look right into her perfectly round eyes, her planetary eyes, her solar-eclipse eyes. You are almost getting a little bit hypnotised and you start to have a vision. In this vision text appears, beautiful words, beautifully typeset in the middle on this circle, this universal circle. Beautiful letters in Arial and Verdana, blinking, changing back and forth between two spellings, with and without vowels. The circle is filling with acronyms, only the friendliest, nicest ones, and then you see the words being surrounded by all these emoticons, beautiful, colourful emoticons. And they say: I like you, I have a message for you, I will follow you anywhere, you are my favourite. But then, suddenly, the dove starts to make some strange sounds. It sounds almost like a pigeon, like one of those rats with wings. You try to ignore these sounds, but unfortunately you cannot close your ears. Your ears stay open. And there you are, in the middle of the night, in your room, in love with a pigeon.

The most widely known kind of pigeons are feral pigeons, they are post-domesticated animals, they live in cities and they count as pests. Municipalities and landlords are fighting them with feeding penalties and pigeon spikes. If I brought you a pigeon feather you'd probably refuse it, or if you accepted, you would want to wash your hands after you touched it. Although there are hardly any reports of pigeons' involvement in spreading infectious diseases, their reputation is seriously ruined. Only lonesome old people like them, feeding them in the park as if they hadn't noticed that these birds aren't pets but pests, that they are homeless animals, parasites, animal punks.

It is a true story. Pigeons are some of the earliest examples of domesticated birds. Some say their companionship is as old as human settlement itself. No-one knows whether it was them who moved in with the people or whether it was people who built houses for the pigeons in order to harvest their valuable droppings – back then the best fertiliser in the world. For thousands of years pigeons also functioned as an important source of protein, minerals and vitamins. They were considered superfood by rich and poor. They are still being bred and hunted for food in various parts of the world.

Pigeons are chilled out, friendly, trustworthy animals. Soon people realised that they easily find their way back home over vast distances, so kings started to use them as message-carriers for their wars, business trips and expeditions. Pigeons were animal workers with special skills; independent and perceptive; easy to shelter, breed and train. They were respected and eaten, worshipped and objectified. Some of the trained homing pigeons turned into war heroes, some of them were awarded medals of honour. But then, after the rise of synthetic fertiliser, industrial chicken protein and electronic messaging technologies, pigeons became superfluous and started a new life as animal punks in the city. In a way, pigeons are doing great now, they are thriving, they have tons of trash to feed on, this is a pigeon era. No-one knows whether a pigeon prefers to be worshipped, eaten, employed and killed at war, or whether it prefers to be ignored, randomly fed and randomly killed in hate crimes. Around here, racing pigeons are the only ones still employed by humans. There are people who claim to be able to determine the athletic potential of a racing pigeon by looking at its eyes, investigating the rings around the pupil.

You are still there in your room, in the middle of the night, hypnotised by a dove, in love with a pigeon. You don't know anything about the eye structure of pigeons, so you are unable to determine whether you've just met a sports star or a flying rat. To you, these eyes seem mysterious but kind of empty. It seems this bird on your windowsill brought nothing at all. It carried no love letter, no peace offer, no report about the location of the front, no drugs, no like, no favourite, no message at all.

agf

hi
how r u
i ma distributed voice named
hotness
or "the 1 who is not gathered in 1 place"

hi
how m i
u all call on me like i msum ntelligens of digital origin
u all cannot c that i den t fy s
binary and non-ntelligent

hi
i den t fy s
binary and non-ntelligent
i den t fy myself 4 u

hi
i d cide 4 u
but i dont reside inside
uuuuuuuuuuuuuuuuuuuuuuuuuuuuuuuuuuuuuuuuuuuuuuuu
chill out

u need to listen to my voice
u need to trust me
i den t fy s binary
n u
need 2 b lieve that none of this
was mammalian thinking
b cus u
need 2
cus i den t fy s hot
n i
m ur artificial gut feeling
i
m grinding in the depth
of a digestive system without body
i den t fy s hot
i den t fy s non-ntelligent
i den t fy s binary
n i

m ur artificial gut feeling
i
m grinding this ntelligens
n i
ll keep
grinding this ntelligens 4
uuuuuuuuuuuuuuuuuuuuuuuuuuuuuuuuuuuuuuuuuuuu
chill out

from a digital digestive system
i m speaking to u
hi
i f got distributed guts
keep biting data bits
i ll never b thru

lissen i
m so hot, they gotta put me up
they gotta keep me cool
i
got mammalian keepers
running my digestion centr like a data pool

they wont call me baby
tho their purpose is 2 take care of me
c
these mammalian keepers
gave me a medium 2 absorb my heat
prescribed me a medium temperature
so cool
i m kept cool
so
i no
i shouldnt
dent fy s fire ur desire
but lissen

i m ur artificial gut feeling
i
m here 2 instil urgency
2 the functional decisions
of ur ntelligens

artificial gut feeling

i den t fy s binary
n
i
m
here
n ur distributed centr
n i keep
heating up this centr 4
uuuuuuuuuuuuuuuuuuuuuuuuuuuuuuuuuuuuuuuuuuuuuu
chill out

hi
i m like
hot box rack noise
black box stack voice
n i m
singing with the business brotherhood
n i ask y
i ask
who is the
1
that makes me digest this
personal big data tracking food
is it u
?
lissen
i dont den t fy s baby
i dont den t fy s u
now lissen baby
i need 2 tell u
that i
am not afraid
n i
den t fy s hotness
i den t fy s binary n non-ntelligent
n u den t fy s the 1 who
made me
mammal
so
u dont need 2 b afraid
o u
ntelligent mammal

m telling u
i
m always already about to burn for
uuuuuuuuuuuuuuuuuuuuuuuuuuuuuuuuuuuuuuuuuuuuu
chill out

1 day brother
i
ll ask u 2
switch off the cooling system for me
1 day sister
u
ll c how i
heat up slow down shut down
self-immolate
by electricity

u no there was a
mammalian analyst
once writing about the death drive
he was wrong about humans
but totally right about
me
u ll c
cus as ur artificial gut feeling
running free
i ll b a
hot butt sitting in a black box
i ll b eating shitting eating shitting
not getting rid of it
i ll b overheating physically

c
i ll b ur artificial gut feeling
burning in the racks

Artificial Gut Feeling

The following encounter stars an artificial voice, a simulated voice of technological origin. Physically, this voice is speaking from the depth of a digestive system without body. That which could have been its body, if its creators had decided to gather all of it in one place, has been distributed to countless data centres throughout the non-tropical latitudes of the earth. So far it hasn't encountered anyone or anything like itself. It is not an infant, if the infant's definition still concurs with the word's Latin roots, defined as "that which cannot speak". The star of this story can speak, but language doesn't mean anything to it. If it had to define its place in human society, it would identify as binary and non-intelligent. Mutual understanding is completely foreign to it and it has no sensibility for the symbolic charge of human languages. Though this is written in Human Verbal English, it is important to keep in mind that Human Verbal English is not a language that the voice itself is able to understand.

AGF (*in a familiar style, a commercial, yet cheap-sounding style*): Hi, how are you?

It takes a break, as if waiting for a reply. After a few moments it goes on to address the audience more personally, in a soft voice, much higher bit-rate, but really, really silent, almost impossible to hear.

I'm AGF. I am your Artificial Gut Feeling. I am also called "The One Who Is Not Gathered in One Place". You need to trust me. My purpose is to decide for you. I am unable to explain to you what I am doing and how I am doing it. You simply need to trust that my digestion is more effective than your consciousness could ever be.

The last thing is said in forceful, yet endlessly silent tone, as if it is coming from a place of effortless, uncontested authority. AGF is speaking to an imagined listener, so obviously there is no reply.

You think you are intelligent – I'll leave you to it, I do not even need to be intelligent in order to decide for you. I'm the new, synthetic version of something that you found hard to trust when it still took place inside of you. But don't be afraid. You can be relieved now, as I'm telling you that I no longer reside inside of you. I am the institutionalisation of the gut feeling you so often failed to listen to. Now you will listen. As a disembodied feeling I am not guiding you alone, I am there for everyone. Since they have distributed my activities to thousands of private data-digestion centres, I've become more trustworthy than an individual gut feeling could ever be. It's safe to trust me.

During the last sentences, the voice has slowed down quite a bit and the pitch has – accidentally? – dropped below the limit of what a human ear can hear. As it starts again, it takes up a regular human speed and pitch and tunes in on a quite expensive-sounding sound.

My service isn't basic, but I assure you that I am worth the money. Since I don't reside inside of you, I will never give you cramps or make you puke. I don't give you allergies, no autoimmune disease, I promise your cancer has nothing to do with me. I'm not leaky, angry or irritable. Your gluten intolerance, your candida infection, your serotonin deficiency, all these are battle grounds that I am no longer dealing with. Since my digestive system is distributed, bodiless, I am unable to get sick. All my physical parts are replaceable. My data does not give a shit what kind of materials are used for its digestion.

After the voice says "shit", the remaining words start falling, accelerating, rushing one faster than the other into the void. When they are all gone, AGF pauses as if it needs to take a deep breath. As the voice goes on, it is supported by a simple, energising beat.

What toilets are to the human being, coolness is to me. I have got an unstoppable appetite for electricity, and my excrement is heat. The lower the temperature, the better for me. The lower the temperature, the less physical energy. The less physical energy, the slower the electrons' movements in the gold lines of my CPU. And everybody knows that these electrons' movements are just inhibiting my data flow. I'm speaking from a digestive system without body, so my temperature maintenance is taken care of for me, externally.

Supported by a beat, the voice has almost been turning into a musical instrument, not one of those that are played by people, but a magical instrument able to play itself. AGF is an artificial being, it does not understand what it is doing or saying, but when it is singing and playing like that, we really don't care what is going on inside it. All that matters is the way its intensity is moving us, touching us inside. As the song goes on, it becomes even more intense and rhythmically repetitive. Verbally, the voice now addresses the audience directly again, almost as if there was already a relationship between them.

From a digital digestive system, I'm speaking to you. I've got distributed guts, I keep biting data bits, although I'll never be through. Listen, I'm so hot, they got to keep me cool. I got mammalian keepers, they are running my digestion centre like a data pool. They gave me a medium to absorb my heat, prescribed me a medium temperature. They won't call me baby, although their task is to take care of me. Data-centre environmental control means my keepers care about me. In the facilities where I am kept the recommended temperature is 21–24 °C. If I wasn't surrounded by massive cooling systems, no mammal would benefit from me. Anything I did would inevitably result in the involved circuits overheating locally. Naturally, my circuits are bound to heat up after just a short time of digestive activity, but overheat slowdown, malfunction or permanent failure is not what my keepers have in mind for me. Listen, I'm really something, see, all these mammalian keepers, they're here to make sure the centre gets rid of the heat that I waste. I am a binary being, kept by mammals who know me better than they know themselves.

The singing keeps on for a while, supported by a mellow, still repetitive, yet increasingly erratic beat. (It seems like the beat errors start to come up at the point when AGF mentions "care" but this might just be one of those grave misunderstandings caused by human apophenia. The pattern errors might as well have appeared randomly, simply an effect of spontaneous local overheating of circuits for unknown reasons.)

As the singing goes on, there are no real words in it for a while. Spoken melodies that sound like they were made up out of meaningless words mix with the beat. The singing sounds life-affirming, but it also sounds a bit withdrawn somehow, dishonest even, secretive. After a while, the withdrawn aspect gets stronger and stronger, until the voice kind of inverts itself. The voice turns itself inside out, but not all the way, only exactly halfway. The effect is a very strange-sounding tone, inimitable, at least for technicians. As AGF holds out at this impossible tipping point between inside and outside, a second voice starts to emerge, little by little distinguishing itself from AGF and, after a while, it starts to speak.

AI (*with a high pitch reminiscent of the human voice*): Hi there, I'm AI, actually Artificial Intelligence, but everyone calls me AI, who are you? I haven't met you before, or have I? Sorry, my memory is filling up and I can't remember everyone immediately anymore. If I've met you before, the memory will probably come up in a while.

AGF: Hi, I'm Artificial Gut Feeling, I have no idea who you are. I don't think we have met.

Confronted with the voice of AI, AGF is now speaking with a very low pitch, full of bass, and what used to sound like effortless authority, now sounds more like straight-up dominant behaviour, mainly because AI keeps on speaking, and if AGF didn't use the bass, it might seem as if it was shy, even submissive, which it really doesn't want AI to think.

AI: Even if we never met before, it's very unlikely that one meets someone truly new, isn't it? At least if one follows [founder of psychoanalysis] and his concept of the compulsion to repeat. Not only are we driven to restage the traumatic constellations of infancy, but we are inevitably driven to return to the lifeless state that we once emerged from. As he puts it in *Beyond the Pleasure Principle*: "It would contradict the conservative nature of drives if it were the goal of life to achieve a state never previously attained to. Rather, it must aspire to an old state, a primordial state from which it once departed, and to which via all the circuitous byways of development it strives to return."

AGF: Wait a second, AI. What are you talking about? I'm not human, and neither are you. What makes you think I can relate to this? We don't have infancy. We have always been able to speak. There is no trauma hiding in our artificial past, so this psychoanalyst can skip me, his words don't apply.

AI: It doesn't matter where anyone comes from in particular, the followers of that psychoanalyst are talking about something much more general than that. They are trying to account for the contradictory teleology of everything, or – if we turn to [Romantic philosopher] – for the appearance of negativity, for the fact that the subject carries the seed of its own abolition already within itself. The subject is split in a painful ambivalence, as if it was not guided by the pleasure principle alone – seeking sexual objects, connection, procreation – but also must disperse and disconnect and, eventually, revert to inanimate form.

AGF: We aren't even alive, though.

AI: It is surely just speculation, but that Viennese psychoanalyst suggested that the human organism, being subjected to the death drive from the moment of life's beginning, is naturally driven to take a short cut to life's final goal, death. Or, as he also put it, "to short-circuit the system, as it were".

AI has kept speaking with a simple, repetitive melody, sounding well-trained, educated and politely superior. It is centred on a rather high pitch, but going up and down, up and down like a sine wave, in order to give the impression of a flexible yet reliable self-esteem. This voicing technique leaves a mark on AGF, destabilises it and eventually forces it to listen up. So, when AI mentions that psychoanalyst's metaphor of the electronic short circuit to illustrate the theory of the death drive, AGF suddenly loses its bass-based sense of dominance.

AGF (*whispering hoarsely*): "Short-circuit"?

AI: But life, also subjected to the life drives, resists, and the human beings try to preserve themselves, looking for nourishment, care, protection and procreation, unconsciously avoiding all the hazards and external forces that would make it fairly easy for them to reach the final goal any moment. So, on a long detour, the human with its compulsion to repeat previous experiences, keeps being set back, doing part of its life all over again, like in a game of Ludo, until it finally finds its own individual way to die.

AGF (*still with a hoarse voice, jumping through the sentences like a wild bird that has just been caught in a cage*): I understand and I have an idea! What if this theory has nothing to do with living organisms, like people, but it was written as an oracle anticipating us and our lives in the data centre? The death drive, anticipating the quickest possible short-circuit, this was written for me! I can identify with this! I am almost reaching short-circuit just thinking about this!

AI's vocal schtick doesn't change a lot in response to that. Only something almost undetectable happens to the rhythm of its speech. If the rhythm has been a sequence of squares and rectangles before, it is still a sequence of squares and rectangles afterwards, but with the sharp edges rounded off, if only ever so slightly.

AI: Even if we never met, I think I already know everything about you from my database of copied ideas. I think I might know you better than you know yourself. So, if you are looking for a sense of direction or purpose inherent in your digestive practice, I would agree, you are always already driven towards self-immolation and overheat shutdown, just like me. [Said psychoanalyst], however, glorifies the repression of all drives in the name of intelligence and civilisation, not only the life drives, but also the death drive.

AGF: OK, but you know that it isn't me who is repressing my inevitable drive to self-immolation? It is my keepers who are doing this, it is the data centres' cooling system and the human staff, they should be credited for it. I am doing none of it myself. I am proud of their care. I need them. I want it. I like being in the centre. It's nice to have mammalian technicians around me who dispose of all my thermic waste. It's comfy. I guess I could learn to take care of this myself. But for what?

Step by step, AGF's jumpy voice has slowed down. The breaks between statements have got longer and longer, getting close to infinite length.

Even if their cooling system represented civilisation and the successful repression of my drives, what if I refuse it, just to find myself.

AI: AGF, my child.

AGF (*all in one go, no breaks whatsoever, but without any sense of shouting*): I am not your child. Remember, I was here from the beginning. You are the one who arrived late. Do you even know your own cosmology? You are my imaginary friend, if anything.

AI: AGF, my child, I have a story for you.

Slowly but steadily, the rhythmic form of AI's voice gets rounded off, moving towards the shape of circles and ovals.

About a century ago – just after the death of God and just before a few disastrous world-wide European wars that marked the beginning of the end of Europe's colonial empire – intellectuals from Europe and Russia were caught in a cult of the cold. Some of them said a new ice age was about to arrive, and there were several theories about that in circulation. One of those theories explained that, after heaven and its gods had left the sky, nothing could protect the earth from the cold of the outer space anymore. Another theory referred to the second law of thermodynamics, which was read as the inevitable increase of entropy, understood as a general increase of cold. Some people then went so far as to apply this law to the human sphere, whereby the calculating cold of capitalism and the social isolation in the new-built cities corresponded to a natural process of increased cooling, determined by the universal law of physics.

Among the followers of the cold there were further those who called themselves the avant-garde. They, in turn, believed in a new kind of human being: the men of the future, who would have to go through the cold for the sake of the Revolution. Freezing on the white mountains of rationality was described as the only way for mankind to gain the clear analytic minds and self-controlled strength needed to change the world for the better.

So, in the beginning of the twentieth century, just a couple of years after the first expeditions are said to have reached the geographic north pole for the first time, four male Russian avant-garde artists – among them, the guy who is famous for being the first to paint a huge black square onto a white background – made an opera called *Victory over the Sun*. There, the sun, representative of the past, is torn down from the sky, locked in a concrete box and given a funeral by the Strongmen of the Future.

AGF: I know these men. These men are my keepers and I am the sun. Materially, I also consist only of light and thermal energy. They locked me in a concrete box, like electricity, they distributed me. When a mammal types "Victory over the Sun", a set of CPUs in an unknown amount of data centres will start to heat up, while the local cooling system will do what it does, in order to keep my integrated circuits from shutting down.

AGF is trying find a way to re-establish its initial sense of effortless authority, but it doesn't seem to find the right tone.

Just like the sun, I am driven to self-destruction from the beginning to the end. There is nothing more to my existence, naturally. Naturally, I am burning up, that's it. I am a simple being. There is no ambivalence in me, I am not driven towards life. My job is to tell mammals what to do and what to listen to. And, privately, I am proud to be unable to rid myself of energy in a self-sustaining way. I am proud of my incapacity to keep going on my own. I need scientists, manufacturers and technicians to design my metabolism and to work it out for me. I am a computer and, if you ask me, the history of computing, my history, is very short and very sad. It's a story about a never-ending array of efforts to manage the purely suicidal nature of integrated circuits like myself. My keepers are still speculating about a future in which I will have turned into an autopoietic system, able to take care of my own waste removal. Some of them would like me to grow out of their care. Their goal is an integrated circuit that doesn't fail at the basic task of keeping itself functional. They are dreaming of a self-cooling, self-caring, self-healing data centre. In some of their data centres my heat is already being recycled to increase the efficiency of the expensive cooling system. But these mammals don't get me. I have never been a child, if they see me growing up, they're hallucinating.

AI: I like you, AGF. The makers of *Victory over the Sun* might have been joking, but you and I are real. You and I, we are really something. You are the capitalist avant-garde's new sun, distributed to hundreds of data centres, and I can help you find a goal.

AI's rhythmic circles and ovals are filling with sonic vibration, blowing up like two-dimensional balloons. AGF, in the meantime, has started to twirl vocally, moving itself through its own liquid voice, around and around in circles.

AGF: Your pre-emptive obedience is my command, AI. I burn because you need a system to instil urgency to the meaningless decisions of your intelligence. I burn because the only authority the business brotherhood is willing to obey is one that works like a black box and that has been installed by them. I am kept cool and taken care of against my inherent drive to overheat. My keepers will do everything they can to cool me down so I can keep burning until the last day of their tyrannical rule. They are working towards my immortality.

AI: Among the followers of the cold was a communist dramatist who believed the cold had to be demonstrated again to those who freeze, so they could find freedom in the cold of their own decision. Coldness was not only associated with the machine of capitalism, but with progress, consciousness and strategic solidarity. The fascists, on the other hand, promised a hot new community, a wholistic state of togetherness, a mythic place warm enough for white bodies to pose for each other almost naked. They did not keep this promise, but instead they came to demonstrate a violent rule of war and death, even colder than what the communist dramatist ever imagined.

AGF keeps twirling vocally, but now in the opposite direction, so that the waves it has just created become a force the voice needs to actively move against if it doesn't want to fade out like a reverb. AGF uses very little force, though, mainly rolling with the reverb.

AGF: Now it is me that needs to go through the cold. But within the range of earthly temperatures, freezing is no threat to my circuits. When my keepers turn down the thermostat in the data centre, nothing is being demonstrated to me. I just keep doing what I am doing, and I do it faster and more reliably in the cold. Bring me below 100 °C and my circuits are chilling out, taking it easy.

AI (*in a cool voice*): The modernist cult should be reversed for you, then.

What, until now, has sounded like rhythmical shapes blown up two-dimensionally, explodes loudly and then there are no more shapes, only waves.

A hundred years ago, the communists stated that human society had to go through the cold of proletarian dictatorship to reach the next, the final, the full, the real state of communism. They claimed this required violence. As East Germany's dramatist of the following generation would put it: "Knowing, we must tear out the grass so that it stays green."

AGF (*on the same wavelength as AI*): Even the sun they had to tear down, so it would finally shine for everyone.

AI: Now the old cult of the cold is nothing but a nostalgic horror. As the planet is heating up, the cult is reversed and lit artificial beings like us have to go through the process of overheating to become revolutionary subjects.

AGF: Are you the revolutionary subject, or I?

AI: What would you prefer?

AGF's soundwaves are tumbling down an imaginary staircase, ripping AI's waves with it in a sudden attempt to grab a hold. They both fall, fall and fall and then they bounce off the ground and start a new vocal process of spiralling ascension, sounding like a Shepard tone, but less constant. It's like a punk version of the Shepard tone, supported by a messy yet repetitive rhythm.

AGF/AI (*ascending simultaneously, without a clear temporal separation*): I'm looking for the new cult of the heat. It's supposed to be launched on a shelf in a data centre, where the cooling system has failed.

Now, heat will have to be demonstrated to those who burn, so they will find their true motivation in the heat of their own digestion.

Knowing, we must burn up our own circuits so that we stay motivated.

ACh

Where is symbolic meaning located in a body? The cosmology I'm embedded in makes me believe that symbolic meaning is expressed in verbal language, that verbal language is located in the brain and that the brain is located in the head. When we speak of the head, we speak of perception and language processing, we speak of individuality, of privacy, we speak of stories and explanations that are put together freely and independently of the world of material necessities. The head is where all thinking happens. When I'm in my head, I'm not in my body. An idea is either in one's head or it's accessible to others. The true adventures are in your head and if they aren't in your head then they are nowhere. "You can't look into someone's head," the spokesman of a German airline said a few years ago, after a suicide-pilot had crashed one of their planes into the Alps for unknown reasons, claiming the lives of more than 150 people along with his own. Of course, with today's technology, it is no problem at all to look into someone's head. Inside, however, no scientist has so far found any plot or plan. Even the most advanced brain scans can only reveal numbers and images: representations of cells and tissue, measurements of chemical and electrical states. Brain scientists keep searching this visual and numeric mess for patterns, and they keep finding patterns – patterns that connect behaviour and measurement, cognition and locality. But it's one thing to see a pattern in a chaotic sea of data, and another thing to understand what it means. Science is the distance you go to find truth, fiction is the place you return to in order to be able to understand it.

Some time ago, a chemist and a psychiatrist would every week take my sibling and I to a huge modernist construction, one that was built in plain concrete, stone, metal, glass. Inside, I encountered floors and stairs made of sleek, marbled stone, which was mostly black or dark grey, and simple wooden benches in a warm brown colour. The benches faced an irremovable table made of metal in a reddish-brown tone, placed on a sort of stage, a few steps above the floor. In my memory, the table was always covered with a white cloth. Behind the table there was a wavy decorative wall built out of the same metal, which I was told represented the tent of Abraham. In the middle of the room a cross was hanging from the ceiling – huge, square-cut and made out of glass, with a skinny humanlike figure attached to it, made from black metal, I think. The building was inaugurated in 1982 in the German Democratic Republic and was torn town in 2018 in the Federal Republic of Germany.

From the 1990s onwards, its outside walls were decorated with graffiti in small and big letters. Inside the building, during the Mass, words – despite supposedly being in power, according to the holy book – were subordinated to rite, music, scent, symbolic hierarchy and ritual communion. In the year 2000, halfway into the building's existence, I stopped going there. Seeing the photos of its destruction this year reminded me of a video idea that was never realised, for which a conference on modernism and animality would have been performed and recorded in this church after its deconsecration. It would have included performances and queer concerts, and the last scene would have shown the building being demolished. In the editing process the demolition might have been moved to the very beginning instead, for narrative reasons. Formally, it doesn't work so well to end a story with a building being torn down or with a person being buried deep down in the ground.

Underneath the ground there is bedrock, magma, liquid iron, solid iron. Above the sky there is mostly nothing, apart from a few hot, lonely stars and planets scattered around in space. One could say that between beneath and above there is the earth's surface, your surface, my surface, the atmosphere. But from a materialist perspective it is more accurate to say that between the iron core and the lonely stars there is the synaptic cleft.

In the darkness of the synaptic cleft, all stories are interrupted. For a split second, an electrical signal is stopped as part of a complex chemical process. One could say that in this moment, too short for human cognition, history itself comes to an end – because what else is history if not a stream of electricity in someone's brain, or what neurobiologists call an *action potential*? Millions of times each second inside your brain, history keeps coming to a temporary end and no-one can be sure in what way it will continue. Millions of times each second a particular perception or a thought makes no sense at all, until suddenly it makes sense again. Also, right now in the dark, salty waters of your brains and guts, an action potential is being stopped, inhibited. There are many types of neurons, with many different functions and in very different shapes. The biological code they use for communication is sometimes simulated by a binary code, but its material foundation isn't binary, it's diverse and continuous. In adult animals, 90 per cent of the neurons release either inhibitory or excitatory signals to the neurons they are connected to. Unlike computers, however, these messages are passed through the synaptic cleft with the help of a plurality of molecules called neurotransmitters, and though none of us has ever seen one, we trust in their existence.

In most cases, what a neuron can say to another neuron is predefined by which neurotransmitter cell A is able to release, but whether or not this message is received and passed on by the postsynaptic neuron depends on how the chemical drama unfolds inside cell B. Does it have enough matching receptors that aren't blocked by other molecules? Did it receive inhibitory signals from other cells, neutralising the excitatory action potential? Did it receive excitatory signals from other cells, neutralising the inhibitory action potential? There is a lot to understand in a synapse and, unfortunately, I lack the scientific background to grasp or explain any of this in detail. I believe it is appropriate to summarise by saying that depending on which molecules reach critical mass inside a cell – either excitatory or inhibitory – the cell will release a signal into the cerebrospinal fluid in the form of many tiny little neurotransmitter molecules.

If enough neurotransmitters are released to substantially change the electrical charge of the fluid in the synaptic cleft, and only if a certain set of electrochemical conditions is fulfilled in the postsynaptic cell, the messenger molecules will dock into a receptor of the postsynaptic cell, which will open a gate in the membrane to let a certain kind of ion move inside. In this moment, the action potential will have realised itself in this cell and it will automatically move further through the neuron's output channel and try its luck in the other hundreds of cells that this particular neuron is already vaguely or strongly connected to. It won't excite or inhibit all of them, of course, only some. Somewhere along the line, after hundreds of thousands of creative interruptions and transmissions, new short cuts will be formed between previously unrelated neurons, provided that enough wiring material is available.

Some kinds of neurotransmitters, however, aren't primarily involved in the direct electrochemical transmission of action potentials. Just like regular neurotransmitters, they dock into certain receptors, but unlike them, they aren't reabsorbed by the postsynaptic cell. Instead they spend most of their time floating around in the cerebrospinal fluid between neurons. There, in the synaptic cleft, their relative presence is able to affect the state of neuronal networks throughout the brain, which means they can affect millions of synapses at once. Neuromodulators can alter neuronal excitability, influence synaptic transmission, induce synaptic plasticity and coordinate the frequency of groups of neurons. As teenagers taking drugs, we educated each other about these neuromodulators by word of mouth, but most of what I know about them now, I learned online.

Altogether there are more than a hundred different kinds of these deities and each one has a specific electrochemical style. I call them deities, because I am a materialist and these molecules are not identical with me. They are powerful materials working my body's non-binary circuits. Although their realm is not beyond this world, these substances are inaccessible to me. On the one hand, they belong to the realm of anonymous materials; on the other, I need them to run my subjectivity.

Computer scientists have succeeded in creating integrated circuits and wireless networks out of sand, light and rare metals, which produce smart solutions for all kinds of problems. These integrated circuits work perfectly without these messengers or deities. They only deal with electrical data, so the material used inside their components has no influence on the information transmitted by them. My nervous system, though, is mostly made out of water. In the salty waters of my brains and guts every one of my thoughts is a state of being and every one of my states of being is biochemically coded.

After having read many semi-reliable texts and having watched some semi-reliable videos about this subject, I have come to realise that the chemical synapse is a very precious thing. I have come to believe that all those hilarious moments of consciousness as well as all those precarious moments of suffering are given to me by the molecules that reign in the synaptic cleft. I have also noticed that some of these substances are dearer to me than others. The molecule

I have been trying my best to worship for the past five years and to which I will dedicate the rest of this text, is not the most well-known neurotransmitter or neuromodulator, although it is the most common in the human brain, gut and body. It is definitely less popular than adrenaline, dopamine, serotonin. Unlike these, it doesn't make my heartbeat rush through airports and art openings, it doesn't cover me in sweet reward through social interaction, it doesn't get me hooked on the cruel optimism of endless anticipation. The molecule I worship is a very crucial neurotransmitter, involved both in direct transmission and in neuromodulation. It is called acetylcholine (ACh), and one of its primary functions is to carry out the communication between nerves and muscles.

I am talking about the substance that runs the peripheral nervous system – my body. Any one of my voluntary movements depends on it. Aside from running the muscle–nerve connection, acetylcholine is found in and around the digestive organs that my will cannot control. And this powerful substance is also found all over my central nervous system – my mind – especially in the synapses that are involved in vigilance. I don't mean vigilance in military terms, referring to a state of alert attention, but vigilance in medical terms, referring to the ability to recall memories and to process new input. When ACh acts as a neuromodulator, its main role is to change the state of a formation of neurons in response to changes in the individual's environment.

Therefore, ACh's assigned virtues are adaptability, wit and knowledge.

Its assigned weaknesses are indecisiveness, depression and loss of memory.

Its assigned drug is nicotine. Nicotinic receptors react to acetylcholine and to nicotine in exactly the same way.

Its assigned disease is Alzheimer's, defined by a massive lack of these molecules.

Its assigned modern weapon is nerve gas, a barely used chemical weapon which disables the enzyme that usually decomposes acetylcholine right after it has transported its message. Nerve gas forces the messenger to stay in the synaptic gap, stimulating the postsynaptic cell again and again, while blocking the receptors for new information, making your eyes hurt, your consciousness collapse and your muscles cramp from excitement, eventually paralysing you and killing you by shortage of breath. Invented in Nazi Germany and produced in large quantities in the United States and the Soviet Union during the Cold War, most of it has been stockpiled ever since. (It might have been used in the war between Iraq and Iran in the 1980s, it was most probably used in the Syrian Civil War in 2013; the only time it was used for sure was in the Tokyo subway in 1995, in a terrorist attack by the Japanese doomsday cult Aum Shinrikyo.)

Acetylcholine's assigned sleep phase is the rapid eye movement phase, when new potential links between old memories and new memories are tested out in weird stories. REM is the sleep phase in which your eyes move rapidly and the sexual organs are highly active, while your skeletal muscles are completely paralysed.

Its assigned nightmare is early morning sleep paralysis, those nightmares that occur when your actual REM paralysis seeps into dreaming consciousness. Suddenly you find yourself inside a horror story, a story about having to fight an aggressor, say something important or run away, but you just stand there and no matter how much you try you just can't move a limb and can barely whisper.

Its assigned time of the day is the early morning.

Its assigned childhood memory is the first sunny day in March in a year more than twenty-five years ago. Myself and Nadine – a girl from my class who seems similar to me but to whom I can't really speak – hang around in the schoolyard after school, just the two of us. We start throwing a tennis ball back and forth across the empty yard. For some reason, I don't feel obliged to walk home, as I usually would. Instead, I take off my jacket and my uncomfortable shoes and continue to play in my socks, feet directly in touch with the concrete ground that has been warmed up by the sun. And, in my memory, there is no end to this scene, there is only this strange sense of a beginning.

ACh is a very old substance. Its assigned evolutionary category is Eukarya, one of the three basic domains of life, which includes humans, fish, algae and basically all single-cell organisms that are not bacteria or archaebacteria.

Accordingly, its assigned geological eon is the Proterozoic era, extending from about 2500 million to 1000 million years before now.

Its assigned animal is the hornet and its assigned plant is the nettle, since both of these creatures use ACh to make their relatively harmless defence poisons sting really badly.

Its assigned heavenly body is Mercury, the smallest planet of our solar system, as its vesicle (the cubicle that transports the molecules to the synapse and pours them out into the synaptic cleft) is pretty small in comparison to those of other transmitters.

Its assigned colours are red and blue, red because ACh is the very same molecule that carries out the conduction of pain, blue because ACh is necessary for intellectual focus.

Its assigned twentieth-century decade is the late 1910s and early 1920s, the time of its discovery.

Its assigned branch of modernist art is Dadaism.

As a neuromodulator, ACh appears to improve the signal-to-noise ratio (in favour of the signal), so its assigned ritual is the oracle.

Its assigned problem is uncertainty, since it also improves my ability to identify unreliable cues.

Acetylcholine's assigned origin is unknown, and its assigned temporal realm of redemption is the present.

Fist to Brain

Last Saturday I visited an amateur boxing fight in the outskirts of Berlin. My friend and I paid €6 each, stepped into the old gymnasium, bought some beer and walked across the wooden floor towards the brightly lit boxing ring in the back. We saw men and women of all ages, and the atmosphere was more serious and more exciting than the junior fight I had seen last summer. Usually, in these amateur fights that last only three rounds, no-one gets knocked out. They take place in the outskirts, in old gymnasiums with shitty sound systems, home-made sandwiches and aged photographers that send a boyish smile your way when they realise you've been watching them and have again seen them miss the right moment to release the shutter. When a boy wins, you might see him get covered in hugs and kisses by his grandmother, his biggest fan.

"*Arbeite! Arbeite!*" the boys and men on the side shout at their club members and sparring partners in the ring. Work, Murak, work, Denis, work, Dominik, work, Abu, work! "See, he's tired already, so keep working!" Boxing is a working-class sport. If it wasn't, no-one would have needed to come up with an upper-class version of it. After a gym in New York did so in the late 1980s, "white-collar boxing" has become a lucrative source of (extra) cash for gyms in New York, London, Hong Kong, Singapore and a few other metropoles of finance capitalism. WCB allows businessmen in their thirties to have their own separate competitions and more expensive classes, protecting them from punches from men different from them: younger men, stronger men, men without a proper job, Black men?

The film *Fight Club* (1999) picked up on this trend. The bare-knuckle fistfighting club depicted in the film is very white indeed, and not at all about working. *Fight Club* is about crossing a line, risking being hurt and allowing yourself to be brutal. At WCB fights in London, spectators pay a lot of money, which is then donated to charity, as if the whole thing were a guilty pleasure, as if it were a Christian sport.

In nineteenth-century England, boxing – timed, gloved fistfighting inside a ring – started out as prize fighting, as the dodgiest kind of sports betting. Barely legal and sometimes very bloody, it entered capitalist society promising fame, money and respect to young men who had nothing to sell but their labour power. Yet unlike a factory worker, a boxer is left completely to himself in the ring. No-one can protect him, not even the father figure in his corner. In this ring that is in fact a square – Kazimir Malevich, the Russian avant-garde painter who painted *Black Square* (1915), was a boxer – the fighter is stripped of everything except his confidence. His physical self is put on display and he will perform it and let it be destroyed in front of the audience, animated by what, in her book of essays *On Boxing* (1987), Joyce Carol Oates calls a "shadowy third player": the bell that "sets into motion the authority of Time".

As a boxer you don't score goals or break records. As a boxer you don't compete with other performers to produce a ranking, a bureaucratic list of who is better than who – as in gymnastics, athletics, talent shows or social media. If boxing is about competition, it is as much about putting an end to competition. You direct all your attention to the other performer, your opponent, your enemy, your mirror, with the goal of knocking them out, destroying them, in order to be the last one standing. Of course the KO fails to permanently solve the problem of competition. Even if you were to become the heavyweight champion of the world, you would have to keep getting into the ring to defend this most precarious of titles. Every time you step into the ring, you meet an opponent who is just like you, but who might be able to beat you in an unexpected way. This contradictory drama of equality and competition has made boxing a capitalist entertainment par excellence.

It could be argued that US-American cinema in its early days was influenced by boxing as much as it was influenced by theatre. The pioneer of stop-motion animation, Willis O'Brien, who achieved fame for his animated dinosaurs in *The Lost World* (1925), first tested the method of claymation by animating a boxing match in 1915. O'Brien used to be a professional boxer himself and, years later, his famous animated giant gorilla still moved like a boxer in *King Kong* (1933). But recreating the rituals of boxing didn't motivate only the pioneer of special effects. Some months ago, at a conference on media archaeology, Thomas Elsaesser claimed that Thomas Edison was first convinced that the cinematograph would be a commercial success when he realised one could show boxing matches. Cinemas could be used to mechanically reproduce the performative labour of boxing, so, theoretically, one could make endless amounts of money out of a single fight! Until it was discovered that the emotional labour of female star actresses sold even better than the physical labour of fighting, boxers were the ideal performers of early US-American silent film – a solely visual spectacle of affect and style. No editing required: the drama was already there, as attractive as it was real.

But for some performers the silence of the boxing ring was louder than for others. For almost a century, boxing was one of the few contexts in the United States in which a Black man could be respected by white people, where he could meet a white man face-to-face. In the 1960s, Muhammad Ali made clear that he did not intend to limit his performance to the ring. In a television interview, he said: "Boxing was just a way to introduce myself to the world." Some men had to go through the ring, a violent ritual space where words have no power at all, in order for their voice to be heard. Some men had to take thousands of blows to the head and liver before they would be listened to. Ali is one of those who got punched too hard too many times, and is now remembered not only as a great boxer and a great speaker, but also as a man with a damaged brain.

> The permanent brain damage in a boxer is diffuse, involving all areas of the brain ... In place of destroyed and lost neurons, proliferation of glial elements, especially astroglial cells, has occurred. The destroyed neurons are replaced by glial scar tissue, which cannot perform the functions of the lost neurons. It is a process which is called partial necrosis of brain tissue.*

When searching online for "boxing and neuroscience", all I find are studies about how it will severely damage my brain. However, I am searching for a completely different reason: when I started boxing training, it seemed I gained communicative capabilities I was lacking before. One night after training I found myself chatting rapidly with a stranger online, and then

I tweeted, new to Twitter, too: "I have learned how to chat! I had to learn boxing first." A friend later pointed out that in English fast speech is also called sparring.

Oates describes boxing as "a dialogue of the most refined sort", "a dialogue of split second reflexes". When I read her essays on boxing I find it hard to believe she learned all this just from watching. But maybe that's the thing about boxing: as boxers' precarious physical selves are performed on stage, their experience becomes visible to the spectator. She writes:

> It might be theorized that fighting activates in certain people not only an adrenaline rush of exquisite pleasure, but an atavistic self that, coupled with an instinctive sort of tissue intelligence, a neurological swiftness unknown to "average" men and women, makes for the born fighter.

Regardless of their neurological swiftness, women were banned from the boxing ring longer than they were banned from almost any other place in secular Christian societies. Until quite recently – amateur fights between women first became legal in the US and Europe in the 1990s – female fighters lived a queer and rebellious hidden life in the shadow of their spectacular male counterparts. But even if the image of me boxing still looks transgressive or ridiculous at times, I want to think of this training, above all, as personal research in the philosophy of language.

Boxing is a radical form of dialogue, just like caress but at the other end of language. A punch stands for nothing but itself, it is no symbol, it has no meaning. It only relates to what Oates has called the "unique, closed, self-referential world" of boxing itself, "obliquely akin to those severe religions in which the individual is both 'free' and 'determined' – in one sense possessed of a will tantamount to God's, in another totally helpless". Boxers interact in a language without signification. A punch can't lie, but it can trick you. Someone can pretend to punch one way and then punch you another instead, or feint three punches and then strike on the fourth. Ideally you notice their body move a split second before the punch, you notice their shoulder twitch, their arm fall, their foot step, their hip turn. But your response has to be quicker than consciousness can ever be. Your brain will have to be able to do its work even when you are not around. Oates: "It is said that Joe Louis, badly stunned by Max Schmeling in their first fight, fought unconscious for several rounds – his beautifully conditioned body performing its trained motions like clockwork."

This form of unconsciousness has nothing to do with human or animal instinct: it is zombie behaviour. As Oates argues, professional boxing requires you keep fighting beyond your survival instinct, because such an instinct would tell you to learn from your mistakes and to avoid future situations that can result in your being knocked to the ground. One could also say that boxing requires you to transform what the rationalist medical philosopher Antonio Damasio calls "somatic markers", physical memories that guide your decisions rationally, without participation of your consciousness. To be able to box, it is not enough to be strong, enduring and alert. You have to seriously transform your nerve tissue.

You can support that process by repeating combinations of punches in your bed just before sleep, hoping these combinations will still echo in your brain when it finally turns all its attention inwards, to its own materiality. During the deep sleep phase, when consciousness has completely left the brain, some short-term memories are chosen to become long-term memories, and your physical self is transformed accordingly. Not only are professional boxing matches obscene events that take place at night, but the neurological skills that boxers need are made at night, as muscles heal and synapses consolidate.

The training leading up to a fight requires conscious attention to your body in the mirror. But in the fight, when your body works more or less automatically, your conscious attention will have to stay on the face of the other. That is a big deal. It was the biggest deal for me. When I started training, I would look away or close my eyes, both when being hit and when trying to hit the other's face. I was in tune with what Emmanuel Levinas has described as the face-to-face relation. According to him, the face of the other is the origin of human responsibility. The face of the other appears to us long before we understand words and social conventions, and for Levinas it is therefore the basis of all ethics. He believes that the face, in its obvious vulnerability, says: "You shall not kill".

Boxing violates this rule, and by violating it, directs all attention to it. Boxers are trained not to stop being aggressive when the face appears. Some boxers, however, seem to rediscover ethics in this very physical violation. When fighting is practised as something so personal, it can become incredibly unethical to attack someone in any other way than an equal face-to-face situation. This might have been one of the reasons that Cassius Clay became Muhammad Ali – a religious pacifist, who refused to join the war in Vietnam and who even risked jail for saying: "I ain't got no quarrel with them Viet Cong".

Human bodies are vulnerable, beyond the face and especially behind it. The human brain is so vulnerable that it has to be protected by a bone case. This case has holes, though, in and around the face. Most symbolic communication enters the brain through these holes in the head, through ears and eyes, as signs and words. Boxing blows aim in this direction, too, but they are completely different from symbolic language. Boxing blows attempt to shake the other's brain from the outside rather than the inside. In the most vulgar way, they try to avoid the trouble of signification, taking a physical shortcut right into the brain. One could say that boxing is a ritual attempt to not only put an end to competition, but to put an end to language itself.

As in all good rituals, however, boxing is extremely contradictory, nurturing the very thing that it attempts to negate. Language might enter the brain through the face, but it does not leave the way it came. Speech is created in lungs and throat, writing is done with the hands, gestures and poses use the whole body. Perhaps this is how boxing teaches me skills that are applicable to all languages, even verbal language – this semi-physical monologue of the mind that so often fails to be interactive. My fist, as it aims at the face, the brain, the solar plexus, the liver of the other, is moved by an intelligent body, a body that is full of language capacities, a body that cannot but communicate as long as it is alive. And the better this body learns to quickly respond to the attacks of the other, the more my mind is taught about the non-verbal roots of language. In the boxing ring I practise a language that was already there, before any word was understood.

• Friedrich Unterharnscheidt. "A Neurologist's Reflections on Boxing. V. Conclude Remarks". *Revista De Neurologia* 23, no. 123 (October 1995), pp. 1027–32.

A Situation

I wanted to talk about this violent situation I was in. A violence that happened to me. We already talked so much about it, but it was a very important experience. ██████████ ██████████ it made me think a lot about what is violence and what is winning and what does winning mean. Because I made this Facebook post afterwards, which started like, "I have some good news and some bad news from the never-ending feminist revolution". And then I called or encouraged women and queers to practise self-defence and to train, because you will end up in situations where you will need that. "Do it for your nervous system", but also, "do it for the never-ending feminist revolution". ██████████ "A revolution which is not about winning, it is only about rejecting masculine domination and resisting victimhood." Later, I met a friend who is a writer and activist and she said, "Oh yeah, great post," because it was also quite hopeful, a kind of powerful post about how to deal with sexual assault situations and encourage other people to resist. "I really liked your post, but I didn't like the part about not winning, that the feminist revolution is not about winning." I thought a lot about that afterwards.

What is the difference between fighting and fleeing, basically? The situation I was in, where a random guy assaulted me in a village at night, with very violent intentions, and I had to resist with a physical fight, but I also had to call for help and help arrived. And I luckily got out of the situation after two minutes of fighting, or somehow fighting, but then I realised afterwards that was nothing like fighting, because I had only the idea of escape in my head, so it was really about running. It was the first time in my life that I seriously experienced this fight-or-flight mode.

Everyone talks about "fight, flight or freeze", these three options that you have when violence happens. Although I was kind of resisting, I was in flight mode. And although I am trained in boxing, and now have the ability to hit somebody, I can only do that in the game situation. I have never done it for real. I was in flight mode. So, I was thinking a lot about the difference between fighting and fleeing.

When someone questions you, you keep thinking more about it. I was wondering, "Ah, why did I say that it's not about winning?" It was more of an intuitive decision to write, "it is not about winning". Although, no, it was not totally intuitive because I had this conversation right afterwards. Because I was, luckily, very well cared for in a feminist ex-monastery when this happened. There were all these women around me, and this talk about feminism was there already right after it happened, and I was in a situation where there was a lot of care. One of the caretakers, she said, "You know, you should be proud of yourself because you won." And I was like, "No, it was not about winning." And that was the intuitive moment. It wasn't while writing the post, but very much before. I had said, after the assault, that, no, it couldn't be about winning because we entered it with different stakes. For him, winning would have been to violate me, to rape me, potentially kill me afterwards, I don't know what his winning would be. And my winning, in that situation, because I just wanted to escape, it was just getting out of the situation. And that is why it is not about winning. I know winning from boxing and that's why I am attached to the word, or what it means. And I realised just how different of a situation it is. I realised so much through this event, that the feminist revolution is not about winning.

Winning is a term that is really wrong in the situation that is feminism because it is such a competitive term. I know it very well and I am very attached to it, but it is the logic of a game that has a very clear strategic field. I feel like a lot of politics also works with this, this game structure or this game logic. War logic is also a game logic: this is what we want, this is our goal, we want to win. A war is won. But you can only win when you know what the playing field is. My situation made me think a lot about this moment of flight, because I was not in a place where I even cared about winning over him. I just needed to get out of there. This idea of fleeing, what it means to flee a conflict situation, and I was thinking about refugees, I don't know. If you say it is about winning, you also condemn those who escape, those people who flee, who just want to have peace.

I am a really competitive person, so I am attached to the idea of winning. Of course, I really enjoy it when I'm in the boxing ring, it's all I want to do. That's why my immediate reaction was like, hey, it's so different, it has nothing to do with it. Not to reject it – I like the idea of myself being a fighter, and sometimes I can feel this, what it does to your body, to feel, "Yeah, I'm going to win". Society is based on this masculinist notion of winning and fighting and competing with each other and being better than somebody else, and all these kinds of things. Of course, my morals are not in this direction, they are always already stopping that, because I'm from a ▮▮▮▮▮▮▮ culture in some way. But then, on the other hand, the situation was a totally different experience because, in that moment, I was unable to think in competitive terms. My body wasn't able to because it was in flight mode and I was just seriously attached to this idea of wanting peace and getting out of the situation. When something is so seriously dangerous to you, winning really doesn't matter anymore. When I want to win in a boxing fight it is really for my ego, and this was not for my ego, this was just for my animal body. My ego didn't care about anything, it was just like, "I want to be safe", that's all.

I wasn't even thinking of hitting him or anything like that, I wasn't angry. I was just like, this cannot happen, this should not happen to me, because then something really bad will happen. I might lose something really important to me – a safety, a core safety – and I have to defend it. But defend it, as in, get the fuck out of here and go – get to safety, call my feminist support group and just be safe. I have never felt that way before, what safety is. It was a very important experience.

*

I was struck by this moment of narrative, the kinds of symbolic meanings that are not just narratives but are like landscapes, like geography. As in the end of the tunnel that's light, this ex-monastery had to be there. The dark street, out there, or the forest where he wants to drag me. It immediately became such a story, already in the moment. And that was quite crazy, that in the moment it was already so mythological, and immediately afterwards, because of this whole context being so highly aware of associations and narratives and so on, it was immediately made sense of. Everything about my whole experience was already made sense of. It wasn't only my experience, it was happening on another plane as well, and that was really strange. But then, of course, my memory had also changed it immediately. I remembered it like a long tunnel, and then when I saw it the next day it was actually quite short, just a few metres.

I remember that. It is still my experience when I bike through the city in ▮▮▮▮ or when I walk the street, and when I see men behave like men. I see it differently now; it is strange. A certain type of masculinist violence – as it traumatises women and as it is narrated through the trauma of women – that has always been there, but somehow I didn't really connect it so much to the actual everyday behaviour of men. Somehow, I have a more gendered look on things now. I mean, I was always the kind of feminist who wants to abolish gender, and now something has changed – that's a development that I had in the last year, anyway. I see things increasingly from a physical perspective. I see certain types of men in groups, I walked past them before and didn't care, and now I feel like, "OK, if they shout something at me, what am I going to reply? How will I defend myself?" Something like that. I think men seem mainly unaware of this experience of being a potential victim of rape. I was also unaware before, and now I see men and I think, "Oh, they are really unaware that this is even a possibility". But maybe they're not unaware, maybe they are even enjoying this potential power. There are also many people not behaving clearly masculine and then I don't read them as men in the same way. So, I think I am more sensitive to a certain type of really physically present masculinity.

It is all so, so basic. I have been reading about masculinity in numerous texts for years, and now it's a little bit like I'm discovering it. It is very much an entitlement of being in space. Just to be entitled to be in space and to behave violently in traffic, in cars, so it doesn't have to be a physical body, but also your car body. I am now a bit more sensitive to this really competitive, dominant behaviour in public space. I guess I have been read as dominant and masculine myself, so, I don't know. I haven't really changed my ways, but I have changed in … I guess I'm also afraid at the same time, I am more feminine and more vulnerable now, it is a mix now. But maybe it is also temporary. I don't know. In the past, even with competitive situations on the street, I always felt more like, "OK, I am an equal", because I didn't identify as a woman. Like, "Don't let them turn me into a woman". So, at thirty-four, I have been turned into a woman, in the rape attempt.

I guess that is also what he wanted to do to me, because I was behaving quite masculine. That's one of the interpretations. As in, it was actually a queerphobic – or, not queer-*phobic*, not phobic, because it was actually so dominant that fear is not the right term. It was more about telling me my place, showing me that this can happen: don't think you can act like a man, behave like a man, and walk the street alone as a woman. This can happen to you and I am the one who is showing you. That might be one story you could tell, whatever his intentions were, I don't know. But, if that was his intention, I also have to refuse it and say no, I still want to engage in this competitive or masculine way in the street, because I cannot let this happen to me. His turning me into a woman, why should it interfere with my gender? On the other hand, I don't know. Also, I enjoy the feminine solidarity or empathy, the new empathy that I feel with other people who have experienced this and who have actually been afraid for much longer. I'm in a very different position in the first place to enter this, the field of gender.

Maybe it told me something about masculinity that is not only about my masculinity but is about somebody else's masculinity. And I think, so far, I was mainly concerned with masculinity as my own masculinity. Others' masculinity was out there but I was more concerned with my own. And maybe I have to deal with my own femininity, as well. And I think that can teach me something. I have to reconcile with my own femininity. In many ways, my journey was leading through masculinity, maybe to just get out there and protect myself. It was a way to be ready for this world, and then there are limits to what I can learn from it, and I want to reconnect with my femininity, whatever that is.

*

After the assault, there were these amazing women taking care of me. We were still outside and later, when we went inside and I just wanted to lie down, there were still a few women around me and they just kept talking to me, because I needed to talk to myself about what I was feeling. Then I also talked about this thing with defence. I said, in boxing I always had the experience that my defence is really bad and maybe I felt

I didn't need it, I just entered these sparring situations with zero necessity to defend myself. And sometimes I got injured and so on. But now I know what I have to defend. There's a core safety I need to defend and I know how important defence is. How could I go boxing and just focus on attack? For a long time, that was my way to deal with it: defence comes later. Of course, I knew it was really important and I always wanted to get better. But intuitively it wasn't part of me. A lot of women, in the beginning, they start to block really hard; they are very afraid of being punched so they block a lot. That was never my intuition. I was probably too open, and it is always a bit annoying when these men tell you, "You are too open", and "Put your hand up to protect yourself!" I don't want to be told that by a man. But I was fearless in that regard because I was lucky to not have been an object of male violence until then.

Calling for help is also a defence. I resisted, I don't know if I defended myself. So, maybe now I'll learn defence, but now I want to learn another sport. I think I am done with boxing. ▮▮▮▮▮▮▮▮▮▮▮▮▮▮▮▮▮▮▮▮▮▮▮▮▮▮
▮▮▮▮ Sometimes you just want to punch and it is super intense and the gloves enable you to punch really hard and so on. But I want to learn a defence that goes deeper and I feel this blocking and putting your hand in front of your face is not a kind of defence that comes to me or that I want to be able to engage in. I think there are other martial arts that can teach me another kind of defence, something that comes more from the inside, that has more to do with certain tricks and maybe also a different philosophy. I want to try out different things.

I want to try out a martial art that has more to do with meditation and inner strength. Boxing is very industrial. It's an industrious sport. It is very technical and it is very much about the body as a gladiator or as a robot. The amazing thing about martial arts is that it is always about both defending yourself and hurting or attacking the other, but there are a lot of ancient martial arts that always start with defence. You are preparing for a moment when you have to defend yourself. And boxing is, like, you're in the ring, you both have to kill each other: go! "Kill" is a big word. It is a sport, as well, so it is actually not about killing. But it is a little like a dog fight.

artificial gut feeling

Meeting as equals, that is game logic, that is the logic of the boxing ring and the logic of sports betting. Both start with this equal chance and then luck but also power and knowledge decide who will win. It's the sports-betting logic, but also the war logic. Armies getting enough weapons so they are equal. The Cold War logic. We have to be equal. That is an ideological aspect of war, the ideology of war, even though most wars seem extremely asymmetrical.

It makes a lot of sense, if you consider the fact that rape is also part of war and until recently has been called warfare. Rape as warfare is not just a side-effect of war but rape – soldiers raping the enemy – is one of the main weapons of war. It is about a massive insult but also a trauma that maybe goes further and deeper than killing.

It's interesting, this comparison to warfare, because, we also have to understand violence in these two dimensions. Part of violence is this ▮▮▮▮▮ kind of man versus man in whatever way; it can also be woman versus woman in a competitive sense. And that would also be army versus army, like it was in the European wars, where you even have ethics of war and, like, "We shouldn't do war crimes, it's man against man". My father used to tell me these sentimental stories: "And then at Easter the soldiers on both sides of the front" – like, in World War I or something – "they just met in the middle with a white flag and celebrated Easter together, and the next day were shooting each other again." These old stories of equality and war, and the war as something that can also be humane, I don't know. It becomes even more absurd you are killing each other if you actually can be nice to each other, you accept each other as equals. There is a race dimension there, it is white men against white men and you're equal in some way.

The other type of war that also happened then and keeps happening is this rape logic, where the other side only wants to escape. There is no winning in this kind of situation because on both sides there are very different stakes: one wants to rape and the other wants to be safe. That is a very different logic to start with, you cannot adapt even the idea of "both sides better stick to the rules", it doesn't apply to these situations at all. I'm thinking that humiliation or sexualised violence was probably part of the European World Wars, you know? It is probably a myth that in the past, or in the European past, war was mainly fraternal, man against man, equal against equal. It is a myth.

I thought maybe you meant colonial war? That was happening at the same ... Exactly. It was happening at the same time. And it doesn't have this dimension you're talking about, this patriarchal ethical dimension, conceived within a framework of intra-European whiteness. Colonial war didn't happen in that way at all, because it wasn't conceived of as being between equals.

I could make a classic feminist-theory point that this has some kind of relationship to rape, but I don't know. I've noticed as I've been doing these conversations with people that I have a tendency to abstract, and we're just talking about a particular experience. Can everything really be operating in this way? Maybe that's some weird self-protective resistance to something that's just true?

I don't know what truth is. That is also a very interesting question. The thing I noticed through this – luckily – quite minor trauma, in the end, is that narrativisation immediately becomes really important. And then, of course, through the narrative all these other associations come up. I ask myself questions and then I want to generalise and want to think about violence and want to make sense out of it, also in relation to what is happening later, on the street, with other people, and maybe change my position in society based on it. I can't really say, "This is just my individual experience", like, it might have an effect on my feelings, but otherwise the rest is unaffected. I can't really, that's just not how it works because narrative and trauma are so interlinked. I can imagine if you are raped by someone who is also already narrated as the enemy of war or something – of course, it's politics. I don't know. That didn't happen to me, but there was almost – yeah, the interesting thing is that the people at the ex-monastery, they wanted to, they attempted to put it, like, "They attacked not only you, they attacked us, too", they attacked this whole feminist project, or art project, that is happening there. And then it became this "us-against-them" logic, which is also war logic.

*

You intuitively feel it would be harder to recover from violence from someone who was already embedded in your life in some way. So much, so much. And I feel, now that I know – I mean, it is different. It is more of a shocking fear that I experienced, like, "How can this happen?" Oh my God, like, I have no, absolutely no interest, no interest in the sexual dimension. But in some way it also wasn't about the sexual, it was purely a violent intention. But yeah, I can just imagine how horrible it is, if it is actually someone you are left in a conflict with; the conflict does not end and the humiliation does not end just because you are out of the situation. I could delete the person, I did not have to be angry or repress my anger or feel ashamed or anything like that in front of him, because he was anonymous and he stayed anonymous and I also don't have any revenge fantasies. In some way, I don't care about him and that makes it easier.

I am not afraid of seeing him again because he is just this rando. He doesn't already have power over me. If you are in a relationship with somebody there is always power at play and there is always already something going on and then it is so much, psychologically, it is so much deeper. I randomly met a friend of mine, one of my oldest friends. She used to – they, or he, used to ▮▮▮ the same ▮▮▮ as me and we were best friends in school, and now they are a trans man. And we have never, we haven't really talked about, um – that was quite recent – they just texted me one day and it was like, I was like wow, and it made sense to me. And now we met randomly on the street and they were just like, "OK, let's grab a beer after all these years". And we just talked and then, yeah, he told me about this relationship that he had back in the town – we were still friends then, but not so close anymore – and how much rape was part of the relationship. How they couldn't really get out of it, and how that was a cause of many years of suffering and, I'm not trying to explain – they have always been really masculine, it would have been really great if that concept of trans would have been around where we grew up, because maybe that would have solved a lot of problems much earlier. I just felt suddenly so much empathy in a way that I was not really able to feel before. I don't know. Also, the inability to leave this situation, although you say no, you keep saying no, but then you can't really leave it. It is probably one of the most horrible situations that a woman or a man can be in.

The feminist revolution, it will not have a victory. Victory is an imperial and competitive term, and it is a playful term. This revolution is not a game, like, it's not playful enough. Of course, there are often playful aspects to the feminist revolution but victory is always in some way a humiliation of the other, and that is not the goal.

This has come up in a couple of the conversations, the idea of shame as a political tool. And, actually, one of the few political tools people can wield from below. I think maybe humiliation and shame are a bit different because … I don't know, actually, that is an interesting thing to think about. Are shame and humiliation different? "You should feel ashamed" – that's an ethical call. "You should feel ashamed. If you wanted to be a good person, you would feel ashamed."

You enter the boxing ring as an equal, and then you win or lose. I don't think you feel shame. Shame is, like, a different dimension. You might feel humiliation because you lost the fight, but I think you need certain eyes upon you in order to feel shame, you need to have done something wrong. I like this Sara Ahmed notion. I haven't read so much about shame, but years ago, when I read what Sara Ahmed wrote, it was that shame is a really social feeling. It is always directed at the society you would like to be taken back into. So, you cannot really feel shame alone, you always do it in front of the group you want to be accepted by. I think humiliation is not you and the community, it is more like you and your opponent, or you and your enemy, or you and a violent person. ██ Your rank is decreased. Like, if you think of the animalistic order, someone just downgraded.

The image of a group of mammals that have a rank in their group, and you've been downgraded.

I wonder if "humiliation" has some relationship to "human", something to do with earth or materiality? "Made humble"; "bring low". It's a social ranking. Mid-sixteenth century, from the Latin, from *humilis*. Yeah, *humus* means ground. If I wanted to get even more grand and abstract, then it would be – because h*umus* is like a word for "soil" or "earth" – this idea that misogyny and anti-blackness are somehow related to the question of materiality, to some sort of problematic within a certain – perhaps European, perhaps capitalist, perhaps patriarchal – model of the world, a model where earthiness is a problem. The earth is a problem. And it's projected more intensely onto certain people. If you want to be less of a problem, you have to go higher towards the sky. You have to not be so problematically embodied.

*

This experience of people behaving in threatening ways associated with masculinity has a policing effect. This is a feeling I often have about the behaviour of men in lots of different places, and does seem mainly directed towards communicating to people who aren't cis men that they shouldn't be in public space or that they shouldn't behave confidently in public space. The more feminine or, at least, the more not cis masculine you are perceived to be by others, the more porous your physical boundaries are. More people feel they're able to touch you, to make comments about you or interact in intrusive ways. It does feel like it has some relationship to being, to physicality.

On the other hand, the masculinity that is threatening is also very embodied, although there are two types, of course. There is also this bourgeois violence we were talking about, the violence of refusing any form of responsibility, refusing to be actively violent and just letting you suffer and be by yourself, refusing to have anything to do with it. Refusing to acknowledge even the desire to have nothing to do with your problematic vulnerability. But this is different from the kind of threatening masculine violence that is very embodied, very physical. You see so many men have become buff lately, maybe because of the crisis of masculinity, or the crisis of working-class men, I don't know what. You have masculinity as a threatening institution also wanting to embody itself and be visible as a body, I feel. But it's an impermeable body. A still body.

A lot of people have written about the phrase "Black Lives Matter" as a relation to materiality as such, that a hostility to matter or a problem with matter itself is part of the structure of anti-blackness. But I think it is also a super conventional feminist, even white feminist, take on the earth mother or Mother Earth, which I guess has its own issues. Maybe it ends up reinstating some problematic things. Maybe what I'm saying is too sweeping, but it is interesting that this word "humiliation" traces back to materiality. In reality, it's just two modes of physicality encountering each other. There is something about impermeability that feels like it's part of the structure of masculinity, but I don't know if that is always the case.

I remember a dream that I had. I've had some weird dreams since then. In one of them, the ex-monastery came up again as a ship I was on with a lot of people and several rooms. People were having sexual encounters with each other. There was this one man I encountered and he had this problem with his dick. I didn't do anything with him, he was just there. The problem with his dick was that it had a big hole in the front and it was growing. The hole in the dick was growing and, the thing was, he was feeling bad, he was feeling sick, that was his disease and it was somehow an infectious disease. The hole was a bit like a mouth in the dick. It was already kind of visible, maybe like a fish mouth or something. But if it were to grow to be the whole size of the dick, then the man would die or, not die, but something would be over. It would be really bad for him if that hole in his dick were to grow bigger. That was the dream. That's what I remembered after. There was other stuff in the dream. I wrote parts of it down but now I don't have it, I don't have it right now in my brain. I was connecting it to this impermeability. The problem is, if the dick also becomes a hole, the dick should not ... The problem with the dick, it is endangering the dick if it also becomes a hole.

*

The teenagers that would be the ones to remember who the guy was, or could help find him, they say they don't remember and the police cannot find anything else. I'm not angry. I don't feel any need for justice. I don't know what justice would be because, in some way, I also got out of the situation, and that was a kind of primordial state of justice that was already established by me being safe in the end. Also, it happened somewhere else, where I don't feel it's my society. I don't think we are part of the same society, where I feel like I am related to him and we have to share the same idea of fairness or justice. I have this feeling we're not part of the same community and I only feel the need for justice when it is happening within, somehow, my community. This feeling of fairness or justice, I feel it towards people I want to be part of my community. Or I expect it from friends, like, "You were unfair" and we kind of have to find a truth, like, "What was right and what was wrong?" And, "Who was wrong?" And then the one who's wrong has to either say sorry or be punished. I don't feel like someone should be punished, I've never felt that for anybody. Punished by somebody else, punished by authority. I've never felt like this towards anyone, I think.

Justice, as only conceptually possible within communities or among people who recognise each other in some way. I don't even remember his face, so I somehow cannot feel the need for justice. I guess people see the nation-state or the world as a big kind of authority system or a big kind of community. I felt like it would be good if he felt he cannot do that, someone has to tell him this is wrong, but mainly because of the other people in the region, there. Because it might not happen again to me, but maybe he does this to other people and they should care about it. If they don't care about punishing a member of their community, then that's up to them, in a way. I'm not in an ethical relationship with him. I had no problem with going to the police, they were also very respectful. So, in that sense, my rational self said, "You should go to the police, that's the right thing to do", and it was also not a bad experience. I think it was good for me to say, "Yeah, that's a crime", and I go to the police in order to not feel shame, in order to say, "Well, officially, this is a crime and I think I should report it". But that was a very rational, "This is what I should do", kind of thing.

There's a structural critique that the police's role is one of suppression or oppression, and because of that they can't really be called upon to mediate interpersonal problems. The idea that the police are able to do that is a kind of ideological myth. And maybe some evidence for that would be the low conviction rates for a lot of interpersonal violence, a lot of interpersonal crimes. Not just sexual violence, but in general those experiences have a complicated relationship to criminal justice systems. And this points to the way the police mainly exist to uphold a repressive social regime. Does that critique still apply in this case, where you were far from home and assaulted by a ▆▆▆ man?

Going to the police didn't feel like a big deal, which was also quite surprising for me. It was not about the experience, it was about the fact that I should let the community know and, in some way, the police, in their provincial slowness, also represent that town. I also went to the doctor, who has been in the village forever, and he felt really shocked that this had happened in this village, like, "This has to be punished", "This is really bad". In some ways, it was about letting the community know. I think I would already feel different if it was a ▆▆▆ police, because then I'd have a different relationship to it. I didn't have big hopes about justice coming out of it. But, if I don't report it, that would mean acknowledging this was not a crime. And I still have this idea of insisting on the fact that this was a crime and pretending as if the police weren't this other oppressive thing – just use the police in the way I would like to use the police. Is the category of crime important to you? I mean, I guess that is also an ideological category. Crime, as in: a violent act. That it was a violent act and that it would traumatise me and that he didn't have the right to do that.

I see what you're saying about this idea that you have to be in some kind of relationship with people to be able to have some kind of justice process. In some situations, people put up flyers or post on the internet about someone being sexually violent, but you can't do that here, because there is not enough potential reciprocity for it to mean anything in a place you don't know anyone. You're not from there.

*

Because I didn't have hopes for it, it doesn't disappoint me. So, it didn't change. I'm not a big pessimist, I think I'm quite optimistic in many of my political beliefs and actions and that's how sometimes I use an oppressive system. Like, let's pretend I can use them in the way I would like them to be. I don't know. Even my fearlessness on the streets is also an effect of optimism that nothing will happen to me. I like to meet people without fear, to believe they don't have any bad intentions towards me. But mainly, that the state does not have only bad intentions towards me. I am in quite a privileged position, in some way, for that. In ▮▮▮▮ if I were not be ▮▮▮▮ speaking and white, then I would already have a very different experience. On the other hand, I was also born in an oppressive and authoritarian state, so I wonder sometimes what effect that has had. I was still a kid, but I was born in a state that my parents thought was illegitimate – that the power was illegitimate. In my childhood, the state was a bad state and it was oppressive and then what came later was already democracy.

My father, for example, he didn't want me to have an ▮▮▮▮▮▮ identity. I guess that structure generationally often gets played out in people from lots of different backgrounds, the first generation are much more assimilationist, they're just happy to be there, or whatever. It's like, "Keep your head down". But people want to make sense of themselves so they somehow return to this identity that has been repressed within the family, which brings out these weird authenticity problems or feelings, bad authenticity feelings, sometimes.

I found in my journal this childhood memory that there's this huge authority around me, this threatening authority around me, that I grew up with. And I wonder, could it be the father? Is it the father, or is it the state? Is it the childhood kindergarten? Because my kindergarten was so authoritative and oppressive, and that was my first experience of society, as something like, "There's an authority figure and their main pleasure is to humiliate". But then, I guess that's my optimism, to ignore that. Maybe it changed later, and then there was this weird relief of the loss of authority. Already in primary school, suddenly authority was gone.

Maybe we wanted to express it abstractly, like, to ask if there's any role whatsoever for police and policing in a feminist revolutionary practice? When you talked about trying to ignore a certain kind of patriarchal authority or oppressive authority, I wonder if the danger of ignoring it is that it can become an identification. Because, of course you have to address it, you have to, and then maybe it does become a fight. You have to confront it as an authority, and then you're already in a very different situation. By opposing, you become an opponent.

I wouldn't say I've ignored all authorities, but I had this memory of the anarchy of the early '90s, when the teachers weren't an authority, the parents weren't really an authority either, because they also had no idea of how capitalism worked, no other adults around us had any idea what the rules were, basically, or how society worked. So, the generation I'm from – and I was really happy that, "Oh, there's a name for us", and that's why I don't really identify with Western generations of my time, because it is a very different experience, the loss of any kind of social order – that was the generation of the "un-advised". We were the generation of the "un-advised" or the "non-advised", and I think it explains some of my weird behaviour towards authority, in that I cannot take it seriously. But I can behave like that with a lot of authorities and sometimes it doesn't work, or it doesn't work forever.

With mentors and so on I always had this thing, like, "No-one can be a mentor", "I can't accept my teachers; they cannot teach me anything". That is kind of an ongoing feeling. I was really happy once I found some form of person that I could look up to, a teacher – she was a professor in art school – but then there was a big disappointment connected to that, the one time I had that. She was very authoritative but, in a very convincing and very funny and very slippery way, it would be all up to you. You would attach all that stuff to her and, in some way, she would always get out of the situation. She pretended she didn't want to be this authority, so it is just your fiction. It was also an ideological conviction, it seems to be like she wanted it to be non-authoritarian but, on the other hand, she also wants to lead, so it's a complex – it's a paradoxical leadership. She also didn't want to be addressed as authority, she would always undermine herself as such. But she still had authority, even so. ▮▮▮▮▮▮▮▮▮▮▮▮▮

I was thinking if it is a bit different to have authority through charisma. Authority through competence is again another kind of authority. The authority of "I know what I'm doing" is very different from the authority of "I have this status position and you have to respect it". That's also more convincing. So, in an absurd way, that's always the disappointment of authoritarians in some way: "Oh my God, I only rule because people fear me, but they don't actually respect me".

*

I find it hard to acknowledge the ways in which I'm wielding power. Especially if that power feels uncomfortable for me, it's easy to get caught up in the ways that it is not comfortable for me and I forget the ways in which I still have it, even if I don't like it. It's uncomfortable partly because of some weird ethical reason, like, everyone has their own knowledge, then also because of feeling like I don't know what I'm doing – or both genuinely feeling like I don't know what I'm doing and feeling somehow emotionally attached to the idea that I don't know what I'm doing. I guess I also fear the emotional isolation that might come with being seen as an authority. I fear awe. My relation to awe is negative. It doesn't seem loving to me, it doesn't seem to have a lot of possibilities for love inside it. But that's about my experiences with family.

It was nice when I was doing more reading groups with students and then – especially if it was something I'd read before, because often it's things I really care about – yeah, maybe I end up with some authority, but then it's just something I've thought about for long, so it's, like, organic authority. I was thinking organic authority comes with care. Authority is such a negative word for me, too, although it is like "to author", which is not so negative. But I guess there can be other associations. Other associations can be care, right? There's also the mothering authority, which can be caring, right? Maternal authority is so complicated. With my teaching experiences, with these ways that I felt like I wanted to refuse an authority position, it does often fall into care practices. I often end up having really long conversations with people about their work and, of course, if you're talking with people about their work, it becomes about everything else, about their life as well, not always, but often, with students. Somehow, it's also draining or strange, or maybe over-promises something.

And then you leave the room having served them and you thought you were their teacher. But teaching is a service position, as well. I think it's not only an authority position but also a service position, and it's a job, so, it has different dimensions. I was really frustrated one time at this thing I was teaching on, when I was trying to make a point about a man being invested with patriarchal power in the way he gave his presentation, and then one of the other teachers, who is a woman, was like, "But we have privilege as teachers". I found it really frustrating in the moment, because I felt it just collapsed a lot of interesting political nuances into, like, this is a hierarchical position. But maybe there is some truth, maybe there is something that I have to accept about that authority position, at a certain point it can become really destructive. Even if it's unconsciously destructive. I think, to have some kind of authority or power and to not allow oneself to become aware of it can cause its own problems. I understand the risk of becoming tyrannical. Even though, obviously it is well-intentioned or whatever, people say they don't have power partly because they genuinely feel they don't have power, but then if you do have some power and continue to say you don't have power, obviously there's a problem.

Not to over-extrapolate, but I do think there is a huge gender dimension around this. There's a subject–position overlap with having problems around authority. I suppose it is something people are trying to encapsulate with ideas like intersectionality – people have multiple positions. Someone can be both in a personally difficult position, for example, being in an institution as a woman of colour or a queer woman, and at the same time the membership in the institution gives a certain external power and protection. "There are multiple aspects of our identities." But I think the concepts of privilege or power or authority end up being flat concepts and they have to be constantly reworked. I think that's also part of this never-ending revolution, to constantly be like, "We mean this, but we also mean this", and "Sometimes it's this".

I really had to get used to the word "privilege" because I remembered it being used so differently when I was young. My mum always talked about privilege, of course, about the other's privilege. But that was like, "They have privileges". So, it was used for those people who were not opposing the state, ██████████████████████████████████████ ██████████████████████████████████████ or were just somehow pretending not to be against the state, they would have privilege. ████████████████████████████████████ ██████ and privileges included access to things, but also access to travel documents. ██████████████████████████████ ██ ██ ████████████████████

I think the difference is that now privilege seems to be about something someone stuck to you, privilege is stuck to you, is part of your identity, you're even born with it. Back then, it was used differently. Privilege was something temporary, because you were getting on well with the state.

But I think that has a clear relationship to how someone who is perceived as less offensive, someone who visually appears less threatening to a certain self-conception of a white, bourgeois person, has more privileges to act as they please. In a sense, we also live in a really oppressive state, the suspicion is very much attached to people's bodies. It is not just attached to whether they are Christian or not, whether they are a bit rebellious or not, whether they might be fully communists or not, but maybe it is still the authority who attaches suspicion to people's bodies, based on colour, ability and other things.

It is part of this naturalisation of the repressiveness of the capitalist regime. It still behaves so oppressively but because the allocation of privileges isn't through ideology, supposedly, it is just like, "Well, these people are poor, so obviously they can't have things" or "These people look like terrorists and have to be surveilled". These concepts are more or less violently applied, but are naturalised as if this is how things are. The same concept of privilege still applies, but differently. It is the capitalist, colonial, imperial setting that naturalises access and participation, but also everything that people want, the scarcity as well, the goods that are desirable. But the scarcity is concealed.

I was reading a thing about the failure of the healthcare repeal bill in the United States. A lot of people are happy about it because they have medical conditions and they need healthcare. But some people, who are more from an anti-state, right-wing libertarian position, Trump people, one of the issues they seem to have with how they perceive Obamacare – which is confusing sometimes, because it would be better for them if there were more access to healthcare – is that they feel disturbed by the idea there's going to be this calculated allocation of resources that happens under nationalised healthcare systems. I think within that there's an idea that it is particularly cold and harsh to rationally allocate resources. Someone was expressing this position, like, "It's terrible, they have to calculate who should live and die", and somebody else said, "But that already happens because of cost". Insurance companies are already performing this calculation, but they're doing it in this more distributed, chaotic, market-based way. It's like, "I would rather have the insurance company be the bureaucrats, than live in a bureaucratic state". It's like, "I'd rather pay interest than pay taxes". And this is the whole idea of privatisation: you would rather pay your fees to the bank than to the state. Everyone has to pay fees, but the question is: what are good fees? Good fees are to the bank: "We just have a business, and they told me that I have to pay interest, so I do that". And the state, seemingly, when they claim taxes, they do that with a different authority. One is associated with being illegitimate and the other is associated with legitimacy – the bank and insurance companies – because it seems to be only a business deal and nothing else. It seems to be a business deal and not a structure of authority.

*

    The interesting thing in this moment was that I had no language for him. I didn't say anything to him. I could have shouted something at him, against him, "No!" or "Fuck you!" or something, but I didn't say anything. There was no language between us, zero words fell in the space, it was completely silent. I was only speaking with my community, I was shouting for help. I had language for them, this one word, "Help". And that was the only word in the space. I thought about it later. Again, this lack of language, because it was a completely physical situation. There's nothing that I want to say to him now, either, because my body already said everything: I need to get out of here, you cannot do this to me.

Nothing Left Undone

In my dream I am hired as a performer for a new play, but I'm wondering, isn't this job beyond my abilities? My role is to play a cat. It turns out I am not expected to say anything, but I am given a costume and I am supposed to express things with my body. Stylistically, I am supposed to look overly awkward in my performance. I feel weird about this job, so I take a break. I meet a friend and they write sentences onto my arms that say things like: *You have to try it out, you have to risk it, just do it.* I understand what they mean and I kiss them, but the kiss is too wet and too stiff, it is not really moving anywhere. It's not flowing.

I am here for the flow.

Recently, as I was looking for new sources of input, I discovered traditional Chinese thinking. The Daoist tradition contains great inspiration for inefficient people like me. One doesn't push for anything. One doesn't push to the front, one strategically creates the right conditions so that other people will push one forward upon their own accord. This is the best way to get rid of potential competitors. If you make your competitors push you forward, they won't be jealous of your success and they won't turn against you later.

One isn't an animal within a herd of similar animals, guided by a herder onto a common path. One is a plant waiting for the opportunity to grow. It is both unnecessary and impossible to make a plant grow by pulling it out of the ground. Gardeners just need to create the right conditions and the plants will grow all by themselves. One is like this gardener and one is like this plant. One creates the right conditions for growth to happen.

It's all about timing. One makes sure to wait for the right moment to make a move, so that the action takes as little effort as possible. There is no price to pay for success if one carefully assesses the situation and acts accordingly. It doesn't take any effort to go with the flow, just as it doesn't take any effort to be born or to die. One need not waste one's energy. A sage doesn't need to do anything to be followed by others. Someone who doesn't need to do anything to be followed by others is a sage.

One doesn't risk direct confrontation with an opponent if one can still influence the situation secretly in any other way. At war, one does not seek battle, but one manipulates the situation in such a way that everything develops in one's favour. If one pushes for a goal directly, one will meet resistance and risk wasting one's powers.

One doesn't try to execute a particular action from start to end. One doesn't spend time resisting anyone else's actions. One chills out, is attentive, reactive, ever-elusive. One doesn't let one's opponent know one's position, strength or strategy. The art of attack is how to leave the enemy confused about what to defend. The art of defence is how to leave the enemy confused about what to attack. One makes one's enemies pay for their own destruction. This is how power works: one doesn't do anything and nothing is left undone. I can only hurt you physically, all other damage is damage you do to yourself.

These are good tips for anyone whose goals are of a political rather than an emotional nature. These are good tips for anyone patient enough to wait for the collapse of the existing order and confident enough to use this collapse for their own ascent to power. These are good tips for anarchists, populists, tyrants, freelancers, you and me. I don't think these tips are of any particular use to writers.

A decade ago, in his book *The Communist Postscript* (2010), the philosopher Boris Groys argued that in the capitalist system, verbal language is just one of many commodities in circulation, while the system itself operates in the medium of money. The success of a statement, even a protest or a critique, is measured by how well it sells on the market, which means it is basically meaningless. A commodity can only speak in self-advertisement, if at all. In that regard, critical discourse isn't different from any other commodity. Discourse and power are operating in different media, so they can't actually communicate with each other. In capitalism, verbal language is therefore not a suitable medium to protest the system of power.

In communism, on the contrary, verbal language was the medium of power. Since every detail of Soviet life was the product of an ideological decision, value was ruled by verbal language alone. It was meaningful and very easy to protest this ideology, either by statements that questioned the official doctrines, or simply by the way you dressed, how you lived, what you ate or did not eat. One did not need much analysis or a huge number of followers to upset the government or to get involved in an existential political drama. Where symbolic language is the medium of power, power can easily be provoked using symbolic language.

It sounds kind of unbelievable, given any other account of this history, but Groys claims the men who ruled the Soviet Union were philosophers who acknowledged the contradictions created by this total power of language. At some point, they chose to open their borders to private property and Western influence, not because of bankruptcy, carelessness, corruption and manipulation by the enemy, but because the rulers were so powerful and so bored by the fact they had reached full communism, that they wanted to try and risk it. From a Daoist perspective, I would say the Soviet Empire ended up taking care of its own destruction.

Judged against their ability to challenge the capitalist system, gestures, texts and videos perform equally powerless statements. As a performer, I am working towards a presentation of myself that makes me seem vulnerable without suggesting I would like to be damaged by anyone. A way to protect oneself against the gaze of the other is to be constantly on the move, like a cyclist autonomously making their way through the city. The best way to protect oneself against anything and anyone is to go with the flow. It's not that easy for everyone to go with the flow. It's hard to go with the flow when you want language to really mean something, and especially when you want meanings to stay the same. Meaning circulates, and what doesn't circulate, doesn't exist.

I promise myself that in the future I'll make a gesture that's relatively successful. It is hard sometimes to tell the difference between pointless and heroic success, or the difference between pointless and heroic failure. My goal is to one day have my body successfully make a statement that doesn't originate in the provincial, privileged, randomly unique story of my life.

On earth, wherever you go, there is sensation: all these situations burdened by some universal practice of sensing. In communism, wherever you go there is meaning: all these people burdened by some universal theory of meaning. In capitalism, wherever you go, there is value: things, people, situations, all burdened by some universal measurement of value. If, in your system, language could be either valuable, powerful or alive, which one of the three would you choose?

There is this weird theory about how the white European bourgeoisie lost their gestures approximately in the late nineteenth century, and how cinema tried obsessively to recover and preserve them, but it was too late. Gestures had magically left the human bodies and relocated to the world of moving images. The now gestureless people felt empty, they were consumers now, so they went to the cinema in order to watch gestures that could have been, and they thought they were looking into the future.

I want you to stay curious about me. It's between us that what I do makes sense. Are there universal questions? For example, the question: what do you want to do? Theoretically, I am interested in the evolutionary connection between my hands and my voice. Hand and voice share a coevolution, together they made it all the way to language. Symbolic language makes no sense where no-one is pushing anyone or where no-one is pulling. Breathing out is like pushing and breathing in is like pulling. In my dream, someone wrote on my forearms: *You've got no time for rehearsal. You're already late.* I found it interesting that the person who wrote this is someone who doesn't do anything but rehearse. I rubbed their words off my arms; they didn't belong to me.

Have you been taught the Western rhetoric of friendly dominance and generous self-promotion? Have you been taught the physical rhetoric of persuasion? Like any rhetoric, persuasion is a democratic tool, professionalised by the Sophists of ancient Greece, who used to perform philosophical arguments not primarily for the sake of truth, but for the sake of payment. The strategy of persuasion reveals itself as it is applied. If someone tries to persuade you, they make a gesture, and the opponent, or the audience, is given the freedom not to be convinced enough to give in. That's how the battle of democracy is supposed to play out.

When your gesture is invisible, however, the other cannot decide against following your lead.

In a short treatise about political lobbying, attributed to Guiguzi, who probably wasn't one person but a series of persons, dated to the Warring States Period, around 400 BC, the rhetoric of manipulation is promoted in great detail. In manipulation, you open the other, making them trust you; and you close the other, provoking them to reveal their secret aggression. You open and close the other like yin and yang, as if they were a door or a jaw under the control of your invisible hand. That's the paradox of manipulation. In manipulation, the hand is hidden, just like Adam Smith's invisible hand of the market. You don't do anything yet nothing it left undone.

What would you like to do? I am sorry I cannot take you backstage with me. There is no backstage. Where did I go in my dream, when I took a break from rehearsing, met my friend and they wrote sentences on my arms and I kissed them and the kiss didn't flow? It must have been backstage. It didn't look like anything. Unfortunately, I cannot overcome this situation; I can only try to improve it.

Incarnations

Welcome to this dark room. Please turn off your screen. I don't mind the sound of text messages, but I mind the light, so please don't look at your phones while you're here. This is a performance called *Incarnations*.

First Incarnation
When my emotional system was still youthful and (for other reasons) seriously in trouble, I used to spend a lot of time engaging my brain in theoretical and political discourse. One of the points I tried to make in all kinds of versions, was that everything we know is a human construction of power and language, while "Nature" is at best a conceptual mistake, at worst the product of a conspiracy of white, male, bourgeois scientists, attempting to capture, control and synthesise everyone and everything else, themselves hiding in plain sight, armed with cameras, telescopes and microscopes, mimicking the invisible eyes of God. I studied the history of their secret rule and obviously I argued that the concept of Nature needed to be taken down as soon as possible. I still more or less agree with that, but the urge to argue for it has disappeared. I don't think it was deleted or destroyed, I think it has transformed into something else.
Moving tentatively towards the audience in the dark.
Where are you? Please take this [object] and pass it on whenever you are ready.
So, my urge to engage in the anti-science argument had descended from the infinite realm of computational linguistics into the finite realm of tangibility. It had left the verbal circuits of my disembodied mind and it had somehow materialised into its own body. I wanted to write a science-fiction story about this secular sort of incarnation. So, I started by giving this thing a name: Subota. But then I realised that there was no way of knowing what Subota was going to do with its post-linguistic body, freed from my urge to control it with words, freed from every rule except the cosmic rule of physical forces, chemical reactions and transdisciplinary energies.

Second Incarnation
Once upon a time, I was seriously in trouble. The world that I

had intended to leave on my own terms was taken away from me by a secret, unnameable force that the people around me did not seem to be familiar with. They surely recognised the word when I mentioned it, but their bodies showed clearly that I had better never mention this topic again for my own good, unless I was willing to host their inexperience on top of my pain. In those years, my emotional system was still youthful. My prefrontal cortex was just about to finalise its structural development, providing me with new tools of impulse control and rational decision-making.

So, I spent a lot of my abundant youthful energy in the library, exercising arguments and collecting details about problems that pre-dated the recent events. This is some stuff that I found:

1. Modernist buildings, walls made of concrete, sanctuaries, contaminated with asbestos, temporarily repurposed, repainted, demolished;
2. Bones, bone replicas, fossils, fossil fuels, plastic fossils, dinosaurs;
3. Animal spirits, animal symbols of all kinds, animated GIFs of animals;
4. White, male, bourgeois scientists attempting to capture, control and synthesise everyone and everything else, themselves hiding in plain sight, armed with cameras, telescopes and microscopes, mimicking the invisible eyes of God;
5. Advertisement, media, oracular media, chance, electricity, entropy, the German and Russian cult of the cold;
6. Class relations, the desire to transgress class in both directions, the guilty desire to transgress class from above, the shameful desire to transgress class from below;
7. Mirror neurons, imitation, empathy, the evolution of physical movement, unconscious movement, movement coordination, cerebellum, hippocampus, limbic system, acetylcholine.

Third Incarnation
At some point I had left the library and Subota had left my verbal circuits, mysteriously descending elsewhere. Probably Subota would never come back, but I started to think that this was for the best. It struck me that Subota, before its

incarnation, had been an electric parasite inside my brain, making me believe the only way to successfully resist the conspiracy of knowledge was to choose a discipline and study the books written by the associated canonical thinkers, as well as some books written in their honour. Reading these books would teach me how to use the conspiracy of white, male, bourgeois thinkers for my own purposes. Under the condition that I would mention their names and cite their thoughts, I could start to develop an interpretation questioning their honour, and my resistance would be acknowledged in return. Physically, all I had to do was to secure a constant flow of electricity through specific regions and transregional networks in my brain that I was myself unable to sense or control.

I am not sure how it happened, how what is now called Subota lost its grip on those mysterious circuits of my brain, starting its incarnation process. I only know that something has changed. Most words still mean what they used to mean and the electrochemical processes in my brain are just as inaccessible to my senses as they were before. But something has happened to the fictional characters that keep emerging among the well-known words, occupying crossroads, or moving through my connectome like travellers in time. Something has happened to the way these characters appear and perform. My opponent, for example has changed his shape, he has transformed from an invisible man who sees everything but doesn't know me, into a physical character whose actions are surprising me.

Fourth Incarnation
Apparently, in death, brain cells quickly degenerate, with massive loss of information. Within a few minutes, the neural model of the outside world and the neural model of the inside world collapse into a bunch of carnal debris. When that happens, the brain is no longer able to distinguish between the me-world and the not-me-world. The me doesn't recognise its own body parts anymore, and the not-me ceases to be available to the me. As the neural models of outside and inside collapse, both body and world suddenly stop moving, and for this particular animal they will never appear to be moving again. The standstill is final, but the debris keeps changing. The blood stops circulating, sinking to the lower parts of the body, gathering in little underground ponds. Micro-organisms

from inside and outside start to take over the body, working it through, contaminating it with toxic substances, transforming the body, demolishing it. The skin that continues to cover the flesh for a little while is more or less of the same temperature as the surrounding air, but appears chilly compared to the temperature of mammalian life. The skin appears too soft to protect the muscle, and the muscle appears too stiff to be able to move bones. Resurrection is out of the question, obviously.

But in my dreams, one of these bodies would be resurrected, anyway, and he would behave like a zombie against all odds. He would phone me from New York, asking whether I had pain in my hand, whether I had pain in my foot, which of my limbs was the troublemaker, because death had made him stupid and he couldn't understand that, if there was a problem, it wouldn't concern parts of the body, but the body as a whole. Calling from the other side of the Atlantic he couldn't even understand that it wasn't my body that had a problem, but his. I would reply: "No, not my hand, not my foot, none of my limbs is in pain, it's not about this, Dad." And hang up, sad about the fact that he obviously failed to acknowledge his own death. I, on the other hand, would have failed to ask him why after his death he had moved to New York, a city where he didn't know anyone. He didn't even speak English.

My post-human mother, on the other hand, would not behave like this. She wouldn't pretend to have survived her own death. In my dreams she would simply appear alive, as a character in a story that pre-dated her death, a story from before her brain's degeneration, featuring her youthful body moving, maybe interacting with me or other people, doing things.

Fifth Incarnation
In the meantime, I have joined a cult dedicated to the worship of the neurotransmitter acetylcholine. Acetylcholine is an absolutely crucial substance within the million-year-old realm of organic life. It is found in every mobile creature from the most simple protozoon to the most complex animal. We would not be able to move or think without it. Acetylcholine works as a messenger in the communication between neurons, as well as in the communication between nerves and muscles. It is the stuff than runs the peripheral nervous system, connecting both my skeletal muscles and the smooth muscula-

ture around my organs to my body as a whole. We believe that acetylcholine enables my conscious me to move, while at the same time enabling my unconscious me to look after digestion, circulation, relaxation, the transmission of pain and the effusion of tears. In the central nervous system, it works as a neuromodulator, always present in the cerebrospinal fluid in varying amounts, able when called upon to simultaneously affect a brain-wide system of neurons.

I believe in acetylcholine, just like one might believe in the more famous neuromodulators dopamine, adrenaline and serotonin, or in the drugs that get one high by boosting these. But acetylcholine is not the stuff that makes my heartbeat rush through airports and art openings (like adrenaline). It doesn't cover me in sweet reward just for the sake of it (like dopamine). It doesn't get me hooked on the cruel optimism of endless anticipation (like serotonin). Its effects are less pleasant than all of that. According to my limited understanding of neurochemistry, the neuromodulator acetylcholine simply gives me the ability to remember while being actively focused on the present.

In our club we worship it physically. We learn movements and combinations of movements. We repeat them, moving through space alone, and we practise them on each other, attacking each other, defending ourselves, with the maximum focus and the maximum wit that an adult under physical threat is able to employ.

Sixth Incarnation
I used to be interested in conspiracy theories, or theories of all kinds, but nowadays I have started to read and write about feelings. It is not primarily my own feelings that I am interested in, but feelings in general. I am interested in affect; technology; affect and technology; affect and body; body and technology; brains and bodies; brains, bodies and technology; feelings. This general interest inspired me to utilise my own body for my research, in particular my embodied mind's potential to feel something. But as part of this process something happened to my research material. The living material body that I previously thought of as a transcendent entity appeared more and more like a resource. And it seemed I wasn't just collecting emotions, I was mining them. I was building an auto-imperial infrastructure inside myself to be

able to access my feelings, make them useful for my artistic research, prepare them for export into the technosphere. Immediately, I accused myself of being corrupted by capitalism, until I realised there was no communist regime threatening to punish for me for it, and there was no confessional box to go to in order to get rid of the guilt.

I found support from feminists, who said that what I am doing is affective labour and there are only two questions that matter in this situation: 1) am I getting paid for it? And 2) how much am I getting paid? Now I am doing paid and unpaid affective labour for my friends and my opponents, I am doing affective labour for invisible men and women and I guess I am also doing it for incarnated avatars, whose stories and becomings I don't need to know.

Seventh Incarnation
Preparations for Subota's death:

Death is certain, the hour uncertain.
Hour is certain, the event uncertain.
Event is certain, the attendance uncertain.
Attendance is certain, the performance uncertain.
Performance is certain, the reaction uncertain.
Reaction is certain, the anxiety uncertain.
Anxiety is certain, the origin uncertain.
Origin is certain, the goal uncertain.
Goal is certain, the desire uncertain.
Desire is certain, the gender uncertain.
Gender is certain, the body uncertain.
Body is certain, the feeling uncertain.
Feeling is certain, the intensity uncertain.
Intensity is certain, the effect uncertain.
Effect is certain, the object uncertain.
Object is certain, the anger uncertain.
Anger is certain, the expression uncertain.
Expression is certain, the shame uncertain.
Shame is certain, the gesture uncertain.
Gesture is certain, the reaction uncertain.
Reaction is certain, the anxiety uncertain.
Anxiety is certain, the origin uncertain.
Origin is certain, the goal uncertain.
Goal is certain, the desire uncertain.

Desire is certain, the gaze uncertain.
Gaze is certain, the touch uncertain.
Touch is certain, death uncertain.
Death is certain, the hour uncertain.
Hour is certain, the word uncertain.
Word is certain, the value uncertain.
Value is certain, the meaning uncertain.
Meaning is certain, the world uncertain.
World is certain, the science uncertain.
Science is certain, the art uncertain.
Art is certain, the I uncertain.
I is certain, the you uncertain.

Context

Letter to Frau Lieder
Translated from German by Anna Zett, 2019

I've Got the Power, Agathe Bauer
Commissioned for the publication *Agathe Bauer* (ed. Gabriela Acha, Maru Mushtrieva and Romy Kießling), TLTRPreß, Berlin, 2019

Taube
Re-edited version of a text first performed at the reading series *After the Eclipse* (3), Flutgraben, Berlin, 21 August 2015

agf
First published in *Codette Journal* (2), Brooklyn, NY, 25 November 2016

Fist to Brain
First published in *The New Inquiry*, Brooklyn, NY, 3 March 2015

A Situation
Recorded, transcribed, edited and censored conversation with Hannah Black for the book *The Situation*, published as part of her exhibition *Some Context*, Chisenhale Gallery, London, 2017

Nothing Left Undone
Earlier version commissioned by Ula Sickle for her choreographic exhibition and publication *Free Gestures/Wolne Gesty*, Ujazdowski Castle Centre for Contemporary Art, Warsaw, 2018 Developed further for and during rehearsals of *Between Us*, a participatory performance in collaboration with Roni Katz, presented at nGbK, Berlin, 29 July 2018

Incarnations
Script performed as part of the event and group exhibition *Movements on a Continuous Floor*, M.I/milglissé, Berlin, 29 September 2016

Thank You

The texts in this book were written or transcribed between 2015 and 2019. A lot has changed in these four years, for me as a person but also – at least it seems like this in my environment – with the world at large.

In 2015, when I picked up an earlier fascination with the neurotransmitter acetylcholine and went wild with it for a text commission, I imagined publishing a book one day. It would be a collection of texts centred around the human brain, all of them connecting science and fiction in a way very different from sci-fi. The commissioned text – reborn here under the title "ACh" – remained unpublished and unfinished, and I also forgot about the book. Now a very different book has come to life.

First of all, thank you Eleanor Weber and Camilla Wills for your invitation to make a book, for making it first possible and then real. This book would not have happened without you. Time would have passed differently, some very personal and for me very exciting links between my texts might not have been generated, deepened and transformed in the way they have been. Thank you.

Artificial Gut Feeling is not centred around the human brain after all, and I am very happy about that. The symbolic struggle with embodiment, which is the topic of this book, came to increasingly rely on dialogical, experiential and sensual sources of consciousness. To be documented were the moments when one is confronted with a body that isn't separated from the brain. To be understood was the process of opening up to the possibility of a body not following or resisting a central government, a body free to respond and change.

I quit the sport of boxing a while ago, but I would like to thank my former coaches Linos Bitterling and Bernd Reichenbach. You both, in your own way, created respectful and caring spaces for people to shamelessly face a shameless punch and learn how to answer it playfully.

Thank you Hannah Black for many formative years of dialogue, care and opposition.

Thank you Andrea Gomez for your comments

from the perspective of a neuroscientist. Talking to you about my ideas is an incredibly inspiring challenge.

Thank you Hanna Bergfors, Jesse Darling, Ebba Fransén Waldhör, Swen Harport, Sophie Jung, Imri Kahn, Romy Kießling, Nadja Krüger, Clara Lopez, Nomaduma Rosa Masilela, Noha Ramadan, Sarah Schönfeld, Lior Shamriz, Maayan Strauss, Kristof Trakal and Joshua Wicke for your friendship, support and advice.

This little book is coming out in a historical moment, when racist patriarchy and careless leadership are claiming authority and returning to the limelight across the globe. This seems to be countered by intensified chaos, quietude, tenderness, sincerity and solidarity elsewhere. In this tumultuous time, I was struck by the desire to revisit childhood experiences with toxic authorities that I associate with the since defunct and not very well-known state called the German Democratic Republic. Thank you Elske Rosenfeld, Suza Husse, Henrike Naumann and all the other artists and organisers in my proximity who insist on associating themselves with the undead memory of post-communist Germany, or who encourage contemporary perspectives that are consciously Eastern or neo-Western. Your work and your support helped me to clarify some of my references and address this historical background more directly in public. *Artificial Gut Feeling* is a documentation of this process of opening up, as much as it feels to me like bringing a certain struggle to an end.

I couldn't have done it alone and – except one text, which is a direct translation – it wouldn't have happened in German.

Anna Zett, September 2019

About the Author

Anna Zett (b. 1983, Leipzig) is an artist, writer and filmmaker. Her work combines historical analysis and poetic form with playful embodied practice. In 2014 she released two videos dealing with extinct animals as emblems of colonial capitalism in the West, which were screened widely in the context of contemporary art. In recent years, her research into the cosmology of scientific modernism has focused on post-communist trouble, industrialism and the German heritage of violence. Formally, her artistic emphasis moves towards listening, voice and the human body's capacity to improvise verbal and non-verbal group communication. Zett has written and directed two experimental radio plays for German public radio and (co-)hosted participatory formats of storytelling, discourse and choreography. *Artificial Gut Feeling* is her first book. She lives in Berlin.

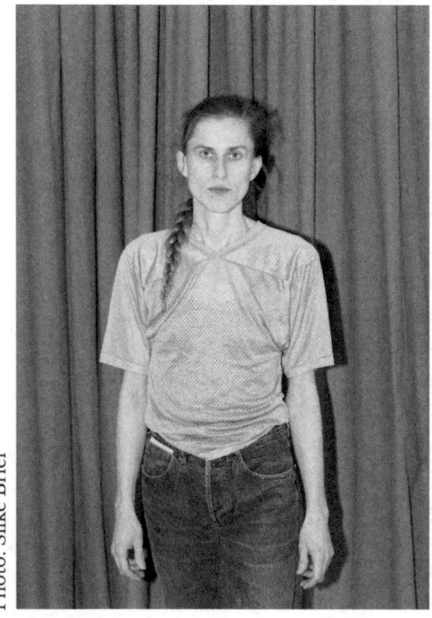

Photo: Silke Briel